RETIRE STRONGER!

YOUR GUIDE TO A HAPPY, FULFILLING
AND WORRY-FREE RETIREMENT

ERIC T. SCOGGINS, CFP®

This book discusses general concepts for retirement and is not intended to provide individualized financial or investment advice. This book is not intended to provide tax or legal advice. Individuals are urged to consult with their tax and legal professionals regarding these issues. Annuities are long-term insurance products primarily designed for retirement income. It is important to know a) that annuities and some of their features have costs associated with them like surrender charges for early withdrawals; b) that annuities used to fund IRAs do not afford any additional measure of tax deferral for the IRA owner; c) that income received from annuities and other assets may be taxable; and d) withdrawals from annuities prior to age 59 ½ may incur an additional 10% IRS tax penalty. It is important to remember that life insurance may require health underwriting and, in many instances, financial underwriting.

Copyright © 2024 by Gradient Positioning Systems, LLC. All rights reserved. No part of this publication may be reproduced, distributed, or transmitted in any form or by any means, electronic or mechanical, including photocopying, recording, or by any information storage and retrieval system, without written permission of the publisher, except in the case of brief quotations embodied in critical reviews and certain other noncommercial uses permitted by copyright law.

Printed in the United States of America

First Printing, 2016

Second Printing, Copyright ©2024

Gradient Positioning Systems, LLC
4105 Lexington Avenue North, Suite 110 Arden Hills, MN 55126
(877) 901-0894

Contributors: Gradient Positioning Systems, LLC.

Gradient Positioning Systems, LLC, ETS Wealth Management, and Eric Scoggins are not affiliated with or endorsed by the Social Security Administration, or any government agency.

TABLE OF CONTENTS

WELCOME TO THE RETIREMENT JOURNEY 1

CHAPTER 1: *WHAT WALL STREET WON'T TELL YOU ABOUT RETIREMENT* 13

CHAPTER 2: *THE TRUTH ABOUT LOSS DURING RETIREMENT* ...25

CHAPTER 3: *ORGANIZING YOUR ASSETS* 33

CHAPTER 4: *WHAT IS THE COLOR OF YOUR MONEY?* 45

CHAPTER 5: *YELLOW MONEY: INVESTMENT STRATEGIES FOR MORE SECURE GROWTH* 57

CHAPTER 6: *A GAME PLAN FOR RISING INCOME* 69

CHAPTER 7: *GETTING THE MOST OUT OF SOCIAL SECURITY* ...75

CHAPTER 8: *CREATING A SOLID INCOME PLAN* 83

CHAPTER 9: *HOW TO CREATE CASH FLOW FOR LIFE* 93

CHAPTER 10: *TAXES IN RETIREMENT*............................105

CHAPTER 11: *TAX ALLOCATION*..................................113

CHAPTER 12: *TAX AVOIDANCE VS. TAX EVASION* 121

CHAPTER 13: *YOU'RE RETIRED...NOW WHAT?* 127

CHAPTER 14: *YOUR LEGACY BEYOND DOLLARS AND CENTS* 137

CHAPTER 15: *CHOOSING A FINANCIAL PROFESSIONAL* 145

WELCOME TO THE RETIREMENT JOURNEY

"Do all the good you can. By all the means you can. In all the ways you can. In all the places you can. At all the times you can. To all the people you can. As long as ever you can."
– John Wesley

As you stand on the threshold of retirement, looking out at what you hope will be your golden years, you want to know that you are doing all the good you can to secure a happy outcome. Most people spend so much time getting TO retirement, they forget to think about how they will get THROUGH retirement. To that end, many worthwhile comparisons can be made between taking a trip of a lifetime and the time in your life called *retirement*. As with any journey, it's not just the destination that matters, it's about enjoying yourself along the way.

» *Gary and Marie had been eagerly planning their Florida road trip for over a year. They were all set with Gary renting a resort condo on a private beach. They were looking forward to relaxing in lounge chairs and sipping on drinks with little paper umbrellas. They will swim in the ocean, stroll along the beach, stay up late and rent movies, sleep in and order room service. Gary had prepared their GPS and loaded his phone with beach tunes and the "Gas Buddy" app to find gas stations enroute. Full of excitement and anticipation, Gary and Marie loaded up the car and back out of the driveway. After more than a year of hoping, dreaming, and planning, they are finally on the road!*

Initially, everything was perfect with music blaring and a picnic lunch on the way. However, trouble began just after noon on their first day when they encountered major road construction. Rerouted into unfamiliar territory, their GPS failed them, and they lost over an hour, they arrived late at the restaurant they planned to eat at that evening, only to discover that it recently went out of business. On cue, it starts to rain. It's really coming down along with great displays of lightning, and Gary misses their next exit. Tired, hungry, and worried about the storm, they drive 20 miles out of their way before they figure out how to get back on track.

They realized they were hours from their hotel on a desolate highway when their fuel light came on. In a "No Service" area, Gary's Gas Buddy app was useless. Turning back to a gas station they'd passed, they found it closed. Tensions escalated as they argued over their predicament, blaming each other

They are tense, and accusations fly back and forth. They say things to each other they maybe should not say, and as the night sky darkens and the rain continues to pour, their dream vacation slowly falls apart.

Like Gary and Marie, numerous individuals enter retirement with excitement but without a concrete plan. You may have investments such as mutual funds, IRAs, and 401(k)s, but do you know how they work together to reach your goals? And what happens when life throws unexpected challenges your way? Running out of gas is inconvenient, but running out of money in retirement is far more daunting.

Many people today make critical mistakes in retirement planning—not due to lack of effort, but because they aren't receiving objective advice for the distribution phase of their financial lives. Many still rely on outdated strategies, ill-suited for today's financial environment. Time poverty and confusion leave Americans uncertain about how to protect their savings and generate income when it matters most. Without financial education, many face retirement with fear, affecting both their relationships and well-being. As I often say, "everything is expensive in the absence of value." Since beginning my career in 1991, and now as CEO of ETS Wealth Management, a fiduciary retirement income planning firm, I am committed to helping people plan wisely for a happy, financially secure retirement.

Focusing solely on your financial health won't make retirement fun or fulfilling if you neglect other key areas: physical, mental, and spiritual well-being. You need a plan for great health in all aspects of life. Wise stewardship isn't just about managing your financial resources but also caring for the nonfinancial areas of your life. This book aims to guide you toward financial independence, so you can retire stronger with enough income and peace of mind. After all, no amount of money matters if you don't have the health to enjoy it.

WHAT ARE THE FINANCIAL PRINCIPLES THAT YOU LIVE BY?

When the Good Lord created this earth, He put into place certain **Physical Principles** that govern our physical world. For example, with Gravity when you jump up in the air, you always come back down. It is a principle, a law, it happens every time you do it. Also, when you wake up in the morning, the sun is always rising in the east, don't look for it to rise in the west, it's not going to happen, it's a physical principle, it's a law.

Similarly, just as the Good Lord put in place physical principles to govern our physical world, He also put in place principles that govern our spiritual world. For example, it's a **Spiritual Principle** where *you will reap what you sow,* love begets love, respect begets respect, and positivity attracts positivity. Just as God instituted these Physical and Spiritual Principles, He also established certain Financial Principles governing our financial world. You can't violate these Financial Principles and expect things to turn out right any more than you can expect to defy gravity.

As good stewards, we have the responsibility to manage and protect the resources that we have been fortunate and diligent enough to accumulate. One problem is that many people misunderstand the financial principles governing investing, which shift dramatically when you move from the accumulation phase to the distribution phase. Retirement is quite unlike any financial challenge you have ever faced before, and today's world demands many different tools and strategies than those of previous generations to Retire Strong!

THIS ISN'T YOUR GRANDDADDY'S RETIREMENT

Retirement planning is more challenging now due to the ever-evolving financial landscape. This book will provide you with a roadmap for combining both proven financial principles with newer strategies to help address the following three major changes:

- **Loss of pension**: Many retiring Boomers rely on Social Security and savings, but lack a guaranteed pension, instead having a 401(k) or similar plan. While these plans allow market participation, they transfer all risk to the investor without providing peace of mind of guaranteed lifetime pension income
- **Global Economy Integration:** The U.S. Stock markets are now more than ever reflective of global events. Unfolding events in China, Europe, or Japan can impact returns for U.S. investors. So don't neglect to consider how geopolitical risk could affect your income, lifestyle, and amount of peace of mind.
- **Longer life expectancies**: Our grandparents who retired may have had it easy when it came to planning, but they also didn't have as many so called "golden years" to enjoy. The life expectancy at birth back in 1930 was a mere 58 years for men and 62 years for women, which meant most people felt lucky just getting to retirement!* The average life expectancy of a 65-year-old couple in the United States is that there's a 50%** chance that one member of the couple will live to age 90, and a 25% chance that one will live to age 95 or beyond. We will discuss tools that will allow you to create your own pension income for you and your spouse's lifetimes if married.

---

* *https://www.ssa.gov/history/lifeexpect.html*
** *U.S. Social Security Administration. (2021). Life Expectancy for Social Security. (https://www.ssa.gov/planners/lifeexpectancy.html)*

GETTING TO VS. GETTING THROUGH RETIREMENT

Although the subject of this book is financial, achieving real success during retirement has more to do with your beliefs and ability to adapt than solely with the accumulation of financial wealth. This might come as a surprise to many because we have been told over and over by the media and Wall Street that it's the SIZE of your account that matters and rate of returns rules all.

Life is a school that presents us with circumstances and situations that allow us to grow, and this growth can help reshape incorrect beliefs, giving us the opportunity to adapt. You might think of the **Law of Life** as, *grow or die*, or, as the U.S. Marine Corps puts it**: improvise, adapt, and overcome.**

Retirement is one such time in your life that requires you to adapt, because the financial principles that got you **TO retirement** are different from the ones that can get you successfully **THROUGH retirement.** During your working years, you are getting TO retirement by working and saving. This is known in the financial industry as *the accumulation phase*. This is the phase you are leaving behind as you enter retirement. Retirement is known as the *distribution phase*. How well you manage this distribution phase is what determines how well you will enjoy getting THROUGH retirement.

There are many risks that retirees face as they enjoy their new longer periods of retirement. Below are a few of them:

- **Wrong Mindset:** One of the biggest mistakes retirees make today is entering the distribution phase with a "growth-centric" mindset and investment strategy. For some the shift can be difficult because they have always maintained this approach during the accumulation phase of their financial life neglecting a plan for safe, effective, and efficient income distribution strategies.

- **Over-Spending:** Putting together a comprehensive income plan before retiring is critical. If you have not created a spending plan and determined what your core expenses and core lifestyle needs are, how can you create a retirement income plan with any certainty that it will meet your needs?

- **Longevity risk:** We talked earlier about the increased life expectancy rates of men and women today. Not only can today's retirees expect to make it to age 65*, but they may still be going strong for many years after. So, it is imperative that you plan wisely and conservatively to ensure that your money will outlast you and your spouse (if married).

- **Inflation:** Growing your investments and income so they can keep up with inflation is always an important retirement income planning consideration. At the writing of this edition, we are enjoying a period of elevated short-term interest rates offered by safe investments such as Money Market accounts and bank CDs because of the "The Fed's" inflation fighting initiatives. However, a more important retirement income planning consideration is; **"how are you going to create a rising income over your retirement lifetime?"** This will be necessary to help offset taxes, inflation and to build wealth for future security including having funds for long-term care costs and legacy goals. The solution requires access to and implementing a full range of investments and rising income strategies which we will cover later in later chapters.

---

* *https://www.rbcwealthmanagement.com/en-us/insights/how-to-plan-your-health-care-and-life-expectancy*

- **Market risk:** Obviously, no one can predict with accuracy when the market will fall or rise. I can promise you, however, that we will continue to see both multiyear bull and multiyear bear markets in the future. Because of this it's imperative to create a **"loss mitigation plan"** to protect against the downside of your investment strategy, as you don't have time at this stage of life to recover from large stock market losses.

- **Rising health care costs:** According to Fidelity Benefits Consulting* in their article titled "How to plan for rising healthcare cost" a couple aged 65 could be facing $315,000 (after tax) on basic healthcare cost in retirement.

  This would include things such as Medicare Premiums, supplemental insurance and other out-of-pocket expenses but EXCLUDING potential home health care, or other Long-Term Care related expenses.

- **Unexpected event risk:** The risk list here includes the loss of a spouse (and one social security & possible pension income), potential Social Security benefit reductions in the future (insolvency risk), long-term care costs, and caring for elderly parents.

  Your "feelings or beliefs" about long-term care may have nothing a to do with the realities of the situation faced by most retirees today. According to the U.S. Department of Health and Human Services, 70 percent of people turning age 65 can expect to use some form of long-term care during their lives.** Also when it comes to our aging parents a good planning question to pose to yourself is

---

* *https://www.fidelity.com/viewpoints/personal-finance/plan-four-rising-health-care-cost*

** *http://longtermcare.gov/basics needs/how much care will you need/*

"am I more likely to receive an inheritance or need to provide financial support to care for a dependent family member?"

Chapter 1 of this book, *What Wall Street Won't Tell You About Retirement*, shows you how the numbers that once worked FOR you during your accumulation years now go to work AGAINST you during your distribution years unless you have a written and implemented a *"comprehensive, holistic, retirement income plan"* in place. Now I know that is a mouthful when I say that so, in our firm, we simply call it the **"ETS Retire Ready Plan"**.

Because of these risks and many others, it's vital to the survival of your nest egg that you both create and implement a *"comprehensive, holistic, retirement income plan"*. Now I know that is a mouthful when I say that so, in our firm, we simply call it the **"ETS Retire Ready Plan"**.

Once you've mapped out your retirement income needs, your written plan must also address these five key roadblocks to a successful retirement:

1. **No** plan to create rising income
2. **No** plan to replace income after a spouse's passing.
3. **No** plan to leverage assets to offset potential long-term home healthcare expenses.
4. **No** plan for a loss mitigation strategy to protect against market losses
5. **No** plan to mitigate taxes on qualified plans and RMD's throughout retirement

This book will share with you how to address these key retirement risks and will encourage you to work with a fiduciary retirement income planning specialist to help create and implement your personal comprehensive plan.

Remember from an investment standpoint, during this season of your life, retirement is **LESS** about capital gain and **MORE** about cash flow. You see, during the accumulation phase the acronym "ROI" stands for **"return on investment"** but during the distribution phase its meaning changes to **"reliability of income."**

It's the CASH flowing into your accounts that keeps the engine of your lifestyle running smoothly and brings tremendous peace of mind. This is why the focus of any good retirement income plan should be on creating guaranteed *"paychecks"* for life to cover any income gaps for your *core lifestyle needs* and at the same time creating *"play-checks"* by using your market-based tools for rising income over your retirement lifetime.

Don't forget it's not the million bucks that will give you peace of mind in retirement, because you can lose those million bucks just as easily as you can lose your way on a dark and rainy highway. It's your cash flow that allows you to enjoy a strong retirement while living happily and financially worry-free, and that is what I am here to help you achieve.

YOUR RETIREMENT GUIDE

What distinguishes a travel agent from a tour guide? Generally, while travel agents provide directions, tour guides lead the way, drawing from firsthand experience. While travel agents often rely on hearsay, tour guides base recommendations on facts, personal experiences and knowledge.

Case in point, during the 2000 tech bubble the financial press proclaimed that tech stocks were the only place to be, and on-line retail was the new economy, while "brick & mortar" retailers were dead. Unfortunately, anyone following that advice of chasing tech stocks following "herd mentality" without considering financial fundamentals experienced incredible losses. My mission since then has been to safeguard retirees from such risks and ensure they have a solid plan including guaranteed income streams with tools that can create rising income and loss mitigation plans or safety nets, sparing them the agonizing stress of financial uncertainty and major losses in the future.

ETS Wealth Management exists to provide individuals and families with innovative investment management solutions. We take pride in the fact that our clients have access to the essential tools to create guaranteed and rising income throughout retirement. Plus, the all-important strategies to grow and protect capital in both good and bad markets. We also offer access to top notch CPAs and Estate Planning Attorneys to create holistic customized retirement plans that allow you to reach your goals and achieve financial independence. When it comes to values, we always do the right thing. And that isn't just a promise, as fiduciaries it's a legal responsibility prioritizing our Client Family Members' interests over our own. While the fiduciary standard of client care is common sense, unfortunately, this principle is not common practice in the financial industry. Generally, speaking, the big banks, brokerages and the local investment franchise on the corner are held to a lower standard of care called best interest that does not require the fiduciary standard in all situations. "Reg BI" (best interest) is often viewed as a middle ground between suitability (the old standard) and fiduciary duty, offering more protection to investors without fully adopting the fiduciary standard. In essence, Reg BI improves the level of care brokers must provide but doesn't reach the same level of strictness as the fiduciary standard.

At ETS Wealth Management we like to say, "is where the Golden Rule *rules*!"

Lastly, I would be remiss if I did not mention that this book consolidates wisdom from many financial mentors as well my own firsthand experiences planning diligently with hundreds upon hundreds of clients since 1991. This helps to equip our team to ensure all our client family members enjoy the best retirement possible. My aim is for all our Client Family Members to achieve a strong, happy and worry-free retirement.

Here's to being golden!

– *Eric Scoggins*, CFP®, Investment Advisor Representative and President E.T.S. Wealth Management

1
WHAT WALL STREET WON'T TELL YOU ABOUT RETIREMENT

If what you thought was always true turned out to be wrong, when would you want to know about it?

Max was born into a middle-class family and had a promising start. Despite being an average student, he had a keen intellect and strong work ethic. After graduating from the University of Georgia in 1985, he pursued the American Dream. By 25, he had a decent job, got married, bought a home, and started a family. Balancing work and family were challenging, but as a DIY'er (do it yourself-er) enthusiast, he took pride in home improvement projects and approached investing similarly. He consistently contributed to his employer's retirement accounts, but with the financial demands of a wife and three children, it wasn't much. Aspiring to retire early, Max absorbed financial advice from various sources—friends, family, colleagues, financial press, and radio shows—*often acting on what sounded sensible, without seeking personal professional guidance.*

Max believed the tech industry was the place to be invested, so he reallocated 100% of his 401(k) to various tech funds, thinking diversification would protect him. Though he didn't fully understand why his investments were thriving, he followed the same advice everyone else did. But in 2000, his financial progress stalled, and he lost 36% of his portfolio in one year. While it was disappointing, he wasn't entirely surprised after years of gains. By October 2001, however, Max was growing anxious with continued losses. Max reminded himself that he wanted to retire before he turned age 60 and sought out some guidance from the local broker and his advisor urged him to stay invested, assuring him it was just a "paper loss" and that he was in it for the "long haul". And who could argue with that?

As the market losses continued, **Max was becoming somewhat of a mental wreck, overwhelmed by conflicting financial advice from TV, radio, friends, family, and his broker.** *He couldn't distinguish fact from fiction and was torn between staying in the market or selling. Sleepless, distracted, and anxious, he even worried about developing ulcers. Who could he trust for advice? Should he call his favorite radio show, and would they take the time to understand his personal situation, retirement goals, fears, and concerns?*

And then one night around 2 a.m., it hits him: Wait a minute, those guys on the radio aren't even licensed to give financial advice, much less able to implement solutions!

It's been said that "Bad breath is better than no breath" but NO advice is better than bad advice!

Money represents more than paper; it reflects your time, talents, and commitments. It meets your needs, supports your lifestyle, and, most importantly, secures your retirement and provides for loved ones after your gone.

You might also have other desires, such as traveling, purchasing property, or moving to be closer to your family (or farther away). The truth is that it takes more than just money to fulfill those needs and desires. Your income, your plans for retirement, your future healthcare expenses, and the continued accumulation of your assets after you stop working and drawing a paycheck all rely on one thing: **You.**

So, what should you be doing with your money?

As the quote at the beginning of this chapter suggests, many people enter retirement making potentially catastrophic mistakes. As they come from their accumulation years, their portfolios are invested heavily in the stock market, in growth-mode investments. Many people like Max are uncomfortable with maintaining this level of risk as they prepare for retirement, and so they start to wonder, "What else should I be doing?" The right answer will depend on your individual situation, the assets you currently own, your goals, risk tolerance and your retirement timeline. That's not the kind of advice you'll hear on the radio, read on the internet, or hear on the news, however.

WHY YOU DON'T WANT TO TAKE FINANCIAL ADVICE FROM THE MEDIA

Free advice is everywhere, but for those like Max nearing retirement, the internet and media often fall short. They discuss investment products broadly, leaving gaps in understanding. Even well-intentioned experts may lack the education, licenses, or experience to give sound advice, and they offer guidance without knowing your personal situation, much like recommending snow tires without knowing the location or vehicle. The biggest issue, however, is the inherent conflict of interest in such advice. The magazines, websites and radio shows are all dispensing information in a biased way—to make a profit. **Their goal is to sell magazines, attract viewers, sell airtime, and sell ads. Their**

goal is NOT to help you design a comprehensive, holistic retirement income plan. They want you to read what they write, listen to what they say and buy what their sponsors recommend *because that's how they make money.*

Those who are planning today for a better financial future by using only free advice from unlicensed, non-professionals such as friends, family and radio personalities are no doubt missing the most effective planning opportunities available today. So called "advice" (in many cases personal opinions) about what to do with money has been around as long as money has existed. While there are basic financial principles that have stood the test of time, most strategies that work adapt to changing conditions in the markets, in the economy and the world, as well as changes in your personal circumstances.

The reality is that investment tools and strategies that may have worked in the past have met challenges in today's economy. Consider, for example, the 4-percent rule many people hear or read about in the media. The 4% rule is how Wall Street recommends people to take income out of their "red" money (all risk assets i.e. stocks & bonds) portfolios during retirement. The 4-percent rule states that if you take out a maximum of 4-percent of your investment account annually, you have a 90% chance of your money lasting 30 years. Those are some good odds.

However, in 2013 there was a Wall Street Journal ad titled ***"Say goodbye to the 4% rule"***. Morningstar Investment Management's 2013 report recommended a maximum safe withdrawal rate of 2.8% from a fully market-exposed portfolio to achieve a 90% chance of your money lasting 30 years. For a $1 million portfolio, this equates to an annual income of $28,000! Yet, even on this modest budget, preserving your principal isn't guaranteed. There are much better ways to secure your retirement income and guarantee that you sleep well at night by using newer and better income strategies that are available in today's financial world. We will explore those a little later.

In today's world of information overload, distinguishing truth from opinion masquerading as free advice is challenging. Misleading phrases like "hold on," "it's only a paper loss," and "you're in it for the long haul" can lead to devastating financial consequences, especially during retirement. The primary reason for this is that those who are either in retirement or approaching retirement simply **do not have the time to make up for large losses in the markets**. This chapter aims to shed light on why a so-called "paper loss" comment is so deceptive and why discernment is crucial.

THE FLAW OF AVERAGES

Like a magician that uses sleight of hand to cover up what is really going on, most brokers on Wall Street have you focused on the wrong thing. They show you *the average rate of return* and sell you on investments based on what they want you to see, but they don't show you the full picture. Imagine you have $100,000 to invest and are given the choice between an investment portfolio that earns 11 percent and one that earns 6.7 percent. Which portfolio would you take?

Most people would sign up for the portfolio that earned 11 percent, and they would lose money. Why? Because they are looking at the wrong thing. What you must ask is, *how did you arrive at that average 11 percent?* Using our example of $100,000, imagine the following three-year scenario:
- Year One: the investment LOSES 50 percent. Now you have $50,000.
- Year Two: the investment GAINS 50 percent. Now you have $75,000.
- Year Three: the investment GAINS 33 percent. Now you have $99,750.

If you do the math, what you have is an average rate of return of 11 percent, yet you actually have LESS money than you started out with!

Now let's look at our second option: a portfolio that averaged 6.7 percent rate of return. Using that same $100,000 investment, consider the following three-year scenario:
- Year One: the investment earns 0 percent. You still have $100,000.
- Year 2: the investment earns 10 percent GAIN. You have $110,000.
- Year 3: the investment earns another 10 percent GAIN. You now have $121,000.

This provides an average rate of return of 6.7 percent. Now, which portfolio would you rather have: the one worth $99,750 or the one worth $121,000?

Losing big during the years just prior to or after retirement is so detrimental to your nest egg, we've devoted Chapter 7 to the reality of how loss affects retirement. But first, let's take a closer look at the myth that says a loss on paper isn't a real loss until you sell the investment.

WHY A PAPER LOSS IS A REAL LOSS

What you need to remember about losses in the stock market is simple: *<u>once you take a loss, you lose the ability to compound interest on that money forever.</u>* It was Albert Einstein who said, "Compound interest is the eighth wonder of the world. He who understands it earns it. He who doesn't, pays it." Let's look at some trickier math to discover why this is true.

Imagine a 10-year time span where "Investor A" earns an average rate of 7.2 percent. One of the most basic financial principles is the Rule of 72 which tells us that at this rate of return, "Investor A" will double his money in 10 years. The math looks like this:

YEAR:	TOTAL:
0	$1,000
1	$1,072
2	$1,149
3	$1,232
4	$1,321
5	$1,416
6	$1,518
7	$1,627
8	$1,744
9	$1,870
10	$2,004

Continue this for another 10 years, and Investor A will have $4,000 in 20 years' time. If you start out with $100,000 instead of just $1,000, you can see how nice it would be to double your money twice in a twenty-year period and end up with $400,000. Now, let's look at what happens to the account balance when our investor loses 8 percent during year three of his growth. That's not an exceptionally large loss, and it only happens once. While the investor doesn't sell and chooses to stay in the market, **this loss drastically changes how the investment compounds its returns.** Look at this math:

YEAR:	TOTAL:
0	$1,000
1	$1,072
2	$1,149
3	$1,057 (-8%)

YEAR:	TOTAL:
4	$1,133
5	$1,215
6	$1,302
7	$1,396
8	$1,497
9	$1,604
10	$1,720

Now our portfolio is worth $1,720 at the end of 10 years instead of $2,000, which means an 8 percent loss in year 3 equates to 14 percent less money in the end. **This loss isn't on paper, folks, it actually results in less money.** If we continue to grow this money for 20 years and never incur a loss again, we end up with $3,440, which is still 14 percent less than what we would have had if that loss in year three never occurred. **Even if you "hold on" and "ride it out" the loss is still REAL.** Add a few more zeros onto the end of the initial investment and you can see why this can be a real problem for retirees who need to rely on their investments for income during retirement. So, the next time you are told "not to worry" about losses in your portfolio because they are only "paper losses" and that you are in it for "the long haul"; you can now dispel this Wall Street myth that has robbed millions of retirees of the ability to achieve their retirement dreams.

If, God forbid next week we entered the next multiyear bear market like the great recession like we had during 2007 through 2009 when the market fell over 50%, do you have any idea how much **your portfolio** could fall by? If the market falls by -21%, -33%, 57% are you simply in the dark about how much risk of loss you are exposed to at this most important season of your financial life? The money that you have accumulated up to this point means more to you now than it has ever meant in your entire lifetime. When do you think would be the right time to know how much risk you're exposed to, before or after the next multiyear bear market? Hopefully you said way before. If you are currently working with a trusted financial advisor my recommendation is to schedule an appointment as soon as possible and pose a couple questions to them:

Question #1: "I know you said that you have us allocated "conservative", "moderate" or "for growth". However, if we were to go through another market, like 2008 or another great recession like market, **what is our loss mitigation plan?** How will we protect the downside?

Question #2: "Based on how you have us currently allocated, and assuming we leave everything deployed, exactly the way you recommend and change nothing and we face another 2008 or great recession, how much can we expect our portfolio to decrease by?

As you can imagine these are **extremely important questions** to ask and get clear answers. Your advisor should be able to provide specific percentages on how much your portfolio might decline based on your current allocation and positions, as well as clearly explain their plan to mitigate losses on your hard-earned money.

After posing these two crucial questions, if you get a deer in the headlight stare, or hear the same worn-out Wall Street rhetoric you've heard all your life" **losses don't matter because they're only on paper, and if you pull out now, you'll never recover, plus you're in it for the long haul,**" then guess what you have just discovered?

That you're working with a broker and not a **fiduciary retirement income planning specialist.** Hear me out there is nothing wrong with brokers. They do a great job of helping people build wealth during the accumulation phase of their lives.

However, the person or persons who may have helped you get TO retirement may or may not be the right person or persons to help you get THROUGH retirement successfully.

A POP-QUIZ FOR YOUR FINANCIAL PROFESSIONAL

At this point, you might be wondering why your financial professional has never shown you math like this before. There is a pop quiz you can give yourself to find out why. Don't worry, it's not a hard quiz; we'll use multiple choice. Ask yourself, **what do you think is the most important question to ask of any financial professional before deciding to trust them with your retirement future?**

#1: How long have you been in the business?
#2: What kind of fees do you charge?
#3: Who do you work for?
#4: What is your golf handicap?

While question number four is meant to be a little joke, most people still fail this quiz. How did you do? Did you guess the answer to be question number two? If you did, you would be wrong. While understanding the fees your financial professional charges is certainly important, **you can really learn everything you need to know about fee structure, experience, and work standards by finding out the answer to question number three:** *Who do you work for?*

In the world of investing and finance, there are basically two different industry standards of client care: the **Suitability** standard or now called **Best Interest** standard and the **Fiduciary standard**.

Suitability standard and Best Interest. If your advisor isn't held to the fiduciary standard, they aren't required to recommend what's best for you at all times. *This allows them to recommend* *products that may benefit them and the company they work for more than you.*

Working for a name-brand company often times limits their product options. If their company lacks what you need, they can't provide it, but they can sell you a less effective option that may generate more revenue for them and their firm. With that being said a step in the right direction came on June 30, 2020, with the Security and Exchange Commission's regulation "Best Interest or Reg BI." Reg BI is often viewed as a middle ground between suitability (the old standard) and fiduciary duty, offering more protection to investors without fully adopting the fiduciary standard. In essence, Reg BI improves the level of care brokers must provide but doesn't reach the same level of strictness as the fiduciary standard.

Fiduciary standard. The fiduciary standard mandates that financial professionals prioritize their clients' interests over their own. Advisor Representatives adhering to this standard must:
1. Always act in your best interest
2. Disclose any conflicts of interest
3. Clarify your investment strategy
4. Align their interests with yours

Typically, independent fiduciary professionals retain greater flexibility by being able to seek out the best investment solutions for you versus only having a limited menu of investment tools offered by their firms. Managing investments requires ongoing customization and adaptation to a changing world. What worked for previous generations may not apply today; retirees and those nearing retirement need newer strategies more suitable for today's financial world and professional guidance.

In summary, here's a quick analogy comparing a broker operating under the new best interest standard of care versus a registered investment advisor operating under the fiduciary standard of care:

Imagine you're buying a car.
A financial advisor operating under **Regulation Best Interest is like a car salesperson** who recommends a car that fits your needs and budget but might also steer you towards one that gives them a better commission, as long as it's still a good option for you. On the other hand, a **fiduciary is like a personal car consultant** who is hired just to find you the best car, with no consideration for their own benefit. The fiduciary's only goal is to get you the best car for your needs, without any hidden motives.

CHAPTER 1 QUICK TIPS //

- Assess whether you're following the right advice on your retirement journey, and don't hesitate to make a financial U-turn if needed.

- Beware of "noise" from the internet, radio, TV, and magazines, often it's just opinion, from those without proper licenses.

- Choose to work with a Retirement Income Planning Professional who held to the Fiduciary Standard.

- Don't overlook creating or understanding your loss mitigation plan to protect your portfolio's downside.

2
THE TRUTH ABOUT LOSS DURING RETIREMENT

"There are two rules of investing:
Rule #1 – Don't lose money. Rule #2 – Never forget Rule #1."
– Warren Buffett

The above quote mentions two investment rules, which this chapter will explain in the context of your distribution years. Generally, there are two types of investors that we see coming through our office: do-it-yourselfers and those who work with the big-name bank and brokerage firms up & down the streets. Interestingly, the investment results we see, and methods used are similar, often relying on buy-and-hold portfolios that are 100% exposed to risk from low to high. So, when the markets are up, they're up when the markets are down they're down in tandem with the market. **There is zero loss mitigation with this approach.**

When the markets go down, the less your portfolio falls the quicker you get back to where you were prior to the market decline. Because of the sequence of returns if you lose 50% in one year, you must make 100% just to get back to even the following year!

This "buy and hold" approach may work well during the accumulation phase of your life as you made regular contributions to your accounts. However, as you transition into retirement (the distribution phase), your strategy must change. Using the same strategies that got you "to retirement" to get "through retirement" increases the risk of outliving your money. During the accumulation phase, dollar cost averaging helps build wealth, as you invest a fixed percentage of your income regardless of market conditions. However, during the distribution phase, withdrawing a fixed percentage from market-based investments, regardless of market conditions, can deplete your savings due to sequence of returns risk and compounded losses when the market declines and withdrawals occur simultaneously. This can jeopardize your lifestyle and cause significant stress, especially during prolonged market downturns.

THE BEST AND THE WORST DAYS OF THE MARKET

Watching the stock market's erratic changes can be stressful, especially when your lifetime of hard work, savings, and investments are at stake. And managing your money alone often brings emotions into play, as market fluctuations represent not just financial changes but a lifetime of effort, so it's hard not to be emotional about it

Everyone knows you should buy low and sell high. It's common sense, but not common practice. This is what is more likely to happen:

The market takes a downturn, like the "Great Recession" from October 2007 to March of 2009 where investors saw the S&P

THE TRUTH ABOUT LOSS DURING RETIREMENT

500 plummet by 57%! They sit paralyzed as they watch their own accounts lose money, month after month, and their retirement dreams fade away. Everywhere they turn, the advice they hear is *"You can't sell now because if you do, you can never earn back the money that was lost."* In fact, as we discussed earlier many brokers will tell you that it's not a "loss" but only a "paper loss" until you sell. I say, "Hogwash!" Once you take a loss, you lose the ability to compound on that money, which means you will need to rely on even larger gains just to get back to where things were before the downturn. At this point most people sell. But eventually, and inevitably, the market begins to rise again. Maybe slowly, maybe with some moderate growth, but by the time the average investor notices an upward trend and wants to buy in again, they have already missed a great deal of the gains.

This is what your broker will point to when trying to convince you of the need to stay in the market. He or she will show you some kind of chart that illustrates just how much money you will forfeit if you miss the best days of the market during a particular period of time.

If they use numbers from Morningstar, they might tell you that from 1990 to the year 2022, the S&P averaged an annual rate of return of 9.83%. Using that time frame, your broker might calculate the following for you:*

IF YOU MISSED THESE DAYS:	THEN YOUR AVERAGE RETURN FELL TO:
BEST 10 days	7.23%
BEST 25 days	4.76%
BEST 50 days	1.63%

---

* *https://www.wealthspire.com/blog/4-reasons-to-stay-invested-for-the-long-run/*

Yikes! With numbers like that, it's no wonder people decide to stay in the market. **A broker looks at the market in terms of keeping you in, so you don't miss the best days.** The broker tells you to stay in the market, so you stay, lose money, and then bite off your fingernails while you hope you can earn that money back again. Your gut is telling you to protect what you have left and not to lose more money, but Wall Street, your broker and the financial media are telling you that it's okay, because you are "in it for the long haul."

Our intrepid investor goes alone, investing without guidance. This approach has two main problems. First, the average investor lacks a proper loss mitigation strategy, often relying on emotion. Second, even those with a disciplined exit strategy to protect their capital may struggle to know when to re-enter the market. Most do not have a disciplined and non-emotional strategy for re-entering the market. They miss the best days. Second, they lose even more money by being in the market during the worst days.

DALBAR's "**Q**uantitative **A**nalysis of **I**nvestor **B**ehavior" study has been used to measure the effects of investors' buying, selling and mutual fund switching decisions since 1994. The QAIB consistently shows that over time **the average investor earns less,** and in many cases, significantly less than the performance of the actual mutual funds they hold. For example, according to DALBAR over the last 30 years, the average asset allocation fund investor earned 2.53% compared to a 50-50 allocation of the S&P 500 and the Bloomberg Barclays aggregate bond index performance of 7.1%.*

Obviously, neither of these investment strategies is an efficient way to be 100% invested in the market during your distribution years when priority number one is generating income. There are more efficient and effective ways for retirees to access market gains

---

* 2022 QAIB, DALBAR Report, January 2023

and at the same time protect the downside through having a **Loss Mitigation Plan**. These strategies can be implemented by having an appropriate portfolio of productive, Red, Green and Yellow money tools.

THE IMPORTANCE OF NOT LOSING MONEY

No one can time the market or predict its best and worst days. However, to illustrate the importance of protecting against losses, let's compare what would happen over the same period if we eliminated the market's worst days:*

IF YOU MISSED THESE DAYS:	THEN YOUR AVERAGE RETURN GREW TO:
WORST 10 days	12.85%
WORST 25 days	15.83%
WORST 50 days	19.79%

As you can see, by missing the worst days, your portfolio stands to gain much more than you might lose by missing the best days. This loss mitigation approach using Yellow money tools, still exposes your portfolio to some market risk however it is managed risk or a defined outcome as you will learn in Chapter 5.

THE RETIREMENT RED ZONE

Earlier, we discussed why using the same rules for accumulating money can harm you during the distribution phase. During accumulation, market highs and lows matter less because you're not relying on your portfolio for income and benefit from dollar cost averaging. In retirement, however, if you don't allocate a sufficient portion of your portfolio to productive Green Money

---

https://www.wealthspire.com/blog/4-reasons-to-stay-invested-for-the-long-run/

tools that first cover your core income needs, you risk more than just market downturns—you could run out of money!

The "Red Zone" is the 5 to 7 years just prior to retiring. During this time, it is critically important to create a comprehensive, holistic, retirement income plan that addresses all of **"The Five Roadblocks"** to a successful retirement. In addition, if your portfolio drops significantly while you are in this zone, you lose the ability to compound your money, and with a large chunk of your savings gone, your money cannot grow at the same rate. As a pre- or post-retiree relying on this money for income, you do not have time to recover those losses. In fact, if you are taking income from your investments and you are experiencing market losses, you are compounding the drawdown (losses) of your portfolio, and you run a much greater risk of running out of money before you run out of life!

Also, expenses such as house payments, unexpected car repairs, and medical bills can force you to sell investments when the market is going down and when you need cash. The worst time for you to sell investments is during a down market. This is why losses during retirement are not just on paper; they affect compounding interest and can cause significant stress unless you have secured your core income needs first.

A better plan is to secure enough guaranteed "Green Money" income and supplement it with a high-quality dividend income portfolio where you live off dividends without selling shares. This will give you the best of both worlds, providing guaranteed income that can be relied on as well as potentially rising income from your market-based Dividend Income Portfolio. In Chapter 6 we will talk more about the benefits of creating a solid dividend income portfolio within your retirement income plan.

Once you've created a comprehensive retirement income plan, secured your core income, established loss mitigation strategies, and addressed the need for rising income with a solid dividend portfolio, you achieve the ideal blend of safety, income, and growth. This ensures a happy and financially worry-free retirement, without fear of another market crash like 2008 or another Great Recession.

You can't control market volatility, but you can use tools to mitigate its negative impact on your overall portfolio and peace of mind. A written income plan addressing **"The Five Roadblocks"** to a successful retirement ensures you won't lose sleep and can enjoy a financially happy and worry-free retirement.

Of course, you will want to regularly review your plan with your fiduciary retirement income planning specialist to ensure it aligns with any changes in your goals, financial situation, health, or risk tolerance.

CHAPTER 2 QUICK TIPS //

- Don't take risks with the money you'll rely on for income during retirement. Secure the funds for your essential retirement income first—the money you'll need every month, no matter how the market performs.

- Consider converting some Red Money investments to Green and Yellow Money to enhance growth potential while mitigating losses.

- Schedule an appointment with a fiduciary retirement specialist to **run a stress test** on your portfolio and assess your risk exposure in a 2008-style market downturn. If your advisor can't provide this, email us at info@etswealth.com for a complimentary consultation, including this and other valuable analyses to ensure you're on track.

3
ORGANIZING YOUR ASSETS

"Improvise, adapt, and overcome." – U.S. Marine Corps

Will your Social Security, savings, and retirement assets be enough? Jeff and Nina wondered the same. At 60, they began thinking about their future—when to retire, what retirement would look like, and how much money they had. They knew they could count on Social Security but weren't sure how much they'd receive or when to file. Jeff had a modest pension available at 67, though he hoped to retire earlier. Nina had a 401(k) but wasn't clear on how it worked or how much income it would provide.

While Jeff and Nina may sound like they're totally in the dark about their retirement, the truth is there are a lot of people just like them. They know retirement is coming and know they have some assets to rely on, but they aren't sure how it will all come together to provide them with retirement income to support their desired lifestyle for the rest of their lives.

You spend your entire working life **hoping** what you put into your retirement accounts will allow you to live comfortably once you clock out of the workforce for good. The key word that can make retirement feel like a looming problem instead of a rewarding stage of life, is *hope*. You hope you'll have enough money. You *hope* you have a wise game plan for turning assets into income to replace those paychecks received while working. While I am a fan of both hope and prayer, when it comes to your retirement, the "hope and pray" plan is not recommended. The Great Recession taught a vital lesson: not understanding investments and how to implement a *loss mitigation plan* can jeopardize your peace of mind, retirement plans and legacies. Saving and investing are necessary, but effective asset management requires careful planning.

THE PURPOSE OF EVERY DOLLAR

From a purely financial perspective, the primary challenge of planning for a long, secure retirement is preparing for the day your paycheck stops and you need to turn a lifetime of savings into income that you do not **outlive** but that will also **rise** over your retirement lifetime to offset taxes, inflation, and build wealth for future security(i.e. leaving a financial legacy, long-term care and home healthcare cost). Retirement income planning is unlike any financial challenge you have faced before. *The money you have accumulated means more to you now than it has ever meant in your entire life.* And retirement is a one-act play. If you get things right, you get to enjoy many years of a comfortable retirement. If you get them wrong, you have a much greater risk of running out of money before you run out of life, so there is a tremendous amount at stake here! Most people who seek advice from a financial professional have done a good job of saving money. They have an investment plan, but not a retirement income plan. *It's* *much more fun to plan for a trip rather than retirement, which is why people spend more time planning their vacations than they do planning for their retirement.* Without a plan, how do you know which bucket of money to draw from first? How do you hedge against inflation? How do you protect your spouse and subsidize their income when you pass away and they lose your Social Security check and the pension amount is cut in half? What if one of you has a home health or long-term care event requiring an assisted living facility or nursing home? Where will you get another $100,375* a year for the average annual cost in Georgia for 2024 to fund long-term care costs?

To build anything lasting, you need a plan, a process, and professional help where expertise is lacking. Just as houses need blueprints, a long-term successful retirement requires careful planning. Your lifestyle, goals, and quality of life shape your retirement strategy. An independent fiduciary advisor, unlike brokers from large institutions, approach retirement planning holistically. As your goals shift from accumulation to preservation, fiduciary guidance becomes crucial to protect against major risks, ensuring your retirement aligns with your desired lifestyle and goals.

The purpose of the money will dictate the placement of the money.

For example, if you want a portion of your core lifestyle income, coming in as a **"Sure Thing"** versus a **"Maybe"** then specific tools designed for that purpose of would be recommended. If inflation is a concern for you then of course you'd want to consider tools that will offer rising income over your retirement lifetime. If covering potential home health or long-term care costs is a priority, your fiduciary advisor can offer alternatives to traditional long-term care insurance, which can be expensive. These plans are often "use

---

* Genworth's Cost of Care Survey

it or lose it" plans, and I can promise you that your premiums will more likely increase for the rest of your life. Alternatively, many life insurance policies and annuities offer riders for increased income in case of chronic illness, known as living benefits. These products provide enhanced income for home health care or nursing home facilities, with the advantage that unused funds remain in your account for your spouse or beneficiary. Even if you're ineligible for traditional long-term care insurance, long-term care riders on annuities and life insurance might still be a viable option for you. These newer tools offer more flexibility than traditional long-term care insurance and are gaining popularity. For these reasons, it's essential to have an open, honest conversation with your fiduciary retirement income planner, so they can recommend solutions that address your top concerns.

SURE THING VS. MAYBE MONEY

Now that you know there's more to saving and planning for retirement than filing for your Social Security benefit and drawing down your 401(k), you can begin to **create a comprehensive, holistic, retirement income, plan AKA the "ETS RETIRE READY PLAN"** that will create significant financial peace of mind after your employer paychecks stop. Understanding how to manage your assets entails risk management, asset diversification, tax allocation and income planning, as well as legacy and estate preparation throughout your life stages.

Let look at some of the basic truths about money as it relates to saving for retirement.

There are two kinds of money: *"Sure Thing"* and *"Maybe."* Everyone can divide their money into these two categories. Some have more of one kind than the other. The goal isn't to eliminate one kind of money but to balance them as you approach retirement.

"Maybe Money" is money that is at risk and provides zero guarantees of principal or income. It fluctuates with the market. It is subject to investor activity, stock and bond prices, market trends, market cycles, geopolitical events, trends, etc.

You get the picture. Due to market volatility, the future value of investments is uncertain, earning it the label it "Maybe Money" vs. a "Sure Thing."

While investing in the market is important, relying on it entirely for the distribution phase of your life is not only risky but simply unwise because future values are unpredictable.

Maybe Money is an important element of a comprehensive retirement income plan because you will still want a portion of your portfolio earmarked for long-term future growth, as well as perhaps investing a portion in a high-quality dividend income portfolio (i.e. ETS Diversified Income Portfolio). The important thing to note here is not to overexpose yourself to market risk because in this season of life because you don't have time to make up for large market losses.

Sure Thing Money, on the other hand, is safer when compared to Maybe Money. Sure Thing Money is made up of dependable, low-risk or no risk money, and tools that you can count on. For example, safe growth tools such as traditional bank accounts, CDs, fixed annuities, fixed indexed annuities, money market accounts, and treasuries would all be considered "Sure Thing" vs. a "Maybe". Sure thing income tools for retirement could include income annuities, and Social Security. These are a couple of the most common forms of income generating "Sure Thing Money" tools.

Knowing the difference between "Sure Thing" and "Maybe" money is a major step towards creating a successful retirement income plan and having the ability to sleep well at night.

HOW MUCH RISK ARE YOU EXPOSED TO?

Many investors don't know how much risk they are exposed to. It is helpful to organize your assets so you can have a clear understanding of how much of your money is at risk and how much of it is in safer holdings. This process starts with listing all your assets to figure out how much is "Sure Thing" and how much is "Maybe" money.

So, let's look at the two kinds of money again:

Maybe Money is, as the name indicates, money that *may* be there when you need it. **Maybe Money** represents what you would like to get out of your investments. Examples of **Maybe Money** include:
- Stocks and Bonds
- Mutual funds, ETF'S, Indexed and Target Date funds
- Variable annuities
- Real Estate Investment Trusts (REIT)

Sure Thing Money is money that you know you can count on. It is safer money that isn't exposed to the level of risk & volatility as the asset types noted above. You can more confidently count on having this money when you need it, and it can't go backwards because the markets go backwards.

Examples of **"Sure Thing" money** are:
- Government backed bonds
- Savings, checking and Money Market accounts
- Pension Income annuities
- CDs
- Fixed Annuities
- Fixed Indexed Annuities

» Sebastian had a modest brokerage account that he added to when he could. When he changed jobs a couple years ago, at age 58, Sebastian transferred his 401(k) assets into an IRA. Just a few years from retirement, he is now beginning to realize that nearly every dollar he has saved for retirement is subject to market risk.

Intuitively, he knows that the time has come to shift some assets to safe alternatives but how much is the right amount?

INTRODUCING THE RULE OF 100

Figuring out your risk tolerance depends on several factors. Your comfort level with investments and your financial advisor's guidance plays crucial roles in aligning your investments with your risk preferences.

Initially, your retirement planning should focus on meeting your day-to-day income requirements. Assessing your core lifestyle expenses and timing are essential steps.

Balancing "Sure Thing" money with "Maybe" money is a prudent strategy, but determining the right mix can be challenging. How much guaranteed income is needed for retirement, and how much risk is acceptable for potential market gains?

To gauge your risk exposure, consider financial principles like the Rule of 100. This rule helps investors strike a balance between risk and security based on their age, goals, and assets.

While "Sure Thing" money offers stability it also brings with it less upside potential. On the other hand, "Maybe" money presents growth opportunities but comes with higher volatility. *Adjusting your risk exposure as you age and your goals evolve is essential for long-term financial security.*

The Rule of 100 provides a good starting point for managing risk and guiding decisions on asset allocation to achieve your financial objectives.

HOW TO APPLY THE RULE OF 100 TO FIND YOUR COMFORT ZONE

The Rule of 100 is a general rule that helps shape asset diversification* for the average investor. The rule states that the number 100 minus an investor's age equals the amount of assets they should have exposed to risk. The important thing to understand here is that the "Rule of 100" is more of a GUIDE than a RULE. Here's how it works:

> **The Rule of 100**: 100 − (your age) = the percentage of your assets that should be exposed to risk (Maybe money)

For a 30-year-old investor, the Rule of 100 suggests focusing on the market and taking more risks, with 70% of your investments exposed to risk.

> 100 − (30 years of age) = 70 percent

Now, not every 30-year-old should have exactly 70 percent of their assets in market-based tools. The Rule of 100 is based on your chronological age, not your "financial age," which could vary based on your investment experience, your aversion or acceptance of risk, and other factors. This rule is a good starting point, though not a definitive solution. After evaluating your risk tolerance with a professional, the Rule of 100 helps adjust your portfolio to match your comfort level.

---

*Asset Diversification disclosure – Diversification and asset allocation do not guarantee better performance or eliminate investment loss risk. Before investing, carefully read the relevant disclosures for each tool you are considering.

ORGANIZING YOUR ASSETS

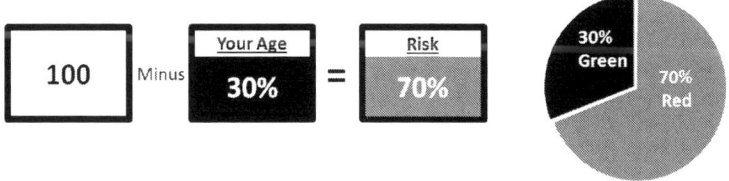

At 30, having 70% of your money in the market made sense due to your time horizon and earning power. Younger investors can take more risks for potential long-term gains. However, risk tolerance decreases with age; losing 30% at 40 offers more recovery time than at 68, when there's less time to recover. The Rule of 100 suggests that an 80-year-old should have no more than 20% of assets at risk, or even less depending on their financial situation. This rule guides risk adjustments with age to safeguard assets, ensure reliable retirement income, and provide financial peace of mind. The Rule of 100 applies broadly to financial management and specific investments like a 401(k), where understanding asset allocation is crucial.

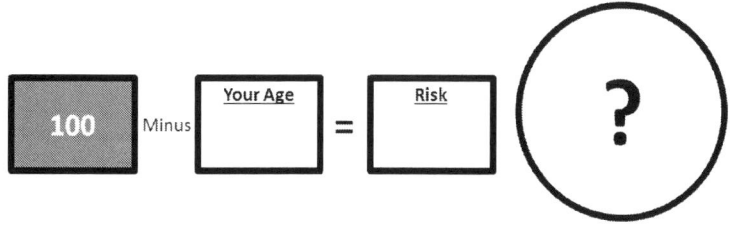

An employer may have someone come in once a year and explain the models and options that employees can choose from, but that's as much guidance as most 401(k) holders get. Many 401(k) options include target date funds that change their risk exposure over time, essentially following a form of the Rule of 100. The problem with that strategy is that it's simply a mix of assets that are **all** still at risk (Maybe Money). Options range from low risk to high risk, but again it's all at some level of market risk or in Red Money. A 401(k) does not offer a plethora of Green or Yellow Money tools.

This is why it's very important if you reach age 59 1/2 to see if your employer will allow moving your 401(k) accumulated balance (tax-free) to your own individual IRA. You're not closing the 401(k); you'll still contribute and receive matching contributions. This will open up the entire financial toolbox available in the industry versus being limited to a menu of 15-30 mutual funds available in your 401(k) or 403(b). **If you need some guidance and help with this type of rollover, our fiduciary advisors will be happy to help make this process easy for you.**

Even if you're under 59 1/2 and locked into a 401(k), our firm can provide a tool to optimize your account with specific fund recommendations based on your risk tolerance. Every quarter you will then receive ongoing proactive recommendations based upon what's happening in the economy and markets. When your allocations need to change, you can then either hit more of the brakes and implement more protection or hit the gas for more growth.

A fiduciary retirement income planning specialist can look at assets in your 401(k) or 403(b) and discuss alternatives to optimize your balance between Sure Thing and Maybe Money.

CHAPTER 3 QUICK TIPS //

- The Rule of 100 is more of a guide than a rule. Your risk tolerance may vary, so consult a **fiduciary retirement income planning specialist** for proper allocation.

- If you're 59 ½ and have a 401(k) or 403(b), contact your plan custodian to confirm if you're eligible for an in-service distribution and can roll your balance into an IRA, offering more "color of money" investment options.

- Embrace change. As you transition from accumulation to distribution, remember "ROI" shifts from "Return on Investment" to "Reliability of Income."

- Just as important as it is to get a **second opinion** on your health, it's also important to get a second opinion on your wealth.

4
WHAT IS THE COLOR OF YOUR MONEY?

*"But divide your investments among many places,
for you do not know what risks might lie ahead."*
— *King Solomon, Ecclesiastes 11:2 NLT*

Over the course of your lifetime, it is likely that you have acquired a variety of assets. Assets can range from money that you have in a savings account or a 401(k), to a pension or an IRA. You have earned money and have made financial decisions based on the best information you had at the time. When viewed as a whole, however, you might not have an overall strategy for the management of your assets. As we have seen, it's more important than ever to know which of your assets are at risk.

Even if you think your 401(k) or IRA is well-funded, not understanding their risk exposure can lead to significant financial setbacks. Consider the Great Recession, where the average diversified stock funds dropped by over 38%.* Some heated advice from a popular radio host during that time, whose professional licensing for investment recommendations is unclear. The host "recommended" the Vanguard Index 500 for its low fees and diversified portfolio of "blue-chip" stocks. However, this "advice" led to devastating losses of over 52% from October 2007 to February 2009!

Sadly, those listeners who took that generic "advice" wound up being "penny wise and pound foolish." Although they may have saved some money in fees, they sat completely paralyzed due to extreme fear as they helplessly watched their dreams of retirement quickly evaporate with their account balances turning those 401(k)s into 201(k)s in what felt like a blink of an eye.

Due to such "advice" and constant conditioning by Wall Street, its army of advisors, the financial magazines and the media it's often main street investors, particularly retirees and pre-retirees, who suffer the most. Again, we're often conditioned that losses in our portfolios are just "paper losses" and won't be realized until we sell (a paper loss is more of a tax concept than an investment concept). Selling "promoted" as weakness, and we're encouraged to stay invested because "were in it for the "long... (go ahead finish it for me)... that's right "haul." This advice sounds logical, but it can be dangerous as we saw the devastating impact of the "Great Recession." Many faced the dilemma of listening to their gut that was screaming "go to the sidelines and protect what you have left" versus Wall Street advice, causing stress, depression, and sleepless nights. Shifting investments away from excessive risk as retirement nears (i.e., the Rule of 100) could have mitigated losses and better protected what took lifetime to build. Remember

---

* *http://www.wsj.com/articles/SB10001424127887324682204578513340507532544*

that "bad breath is better than no breath," but NO ADVICE is certainly better than bad advice!

One of the easiest ways to understand the risk inside your current investment portfolio is to use a color system for your money.

THE COLOR OF MONEY

We use the colors red, yellow, and green to identify the different levels of risk your investments are exposed to. Each color has unique benefits and features.

- **Green Money** prioritizes safety, offering either a guaranteed principal or lifetime income. While no investment is entirely risk-free, these strategies focus on protecting the principal or income in retirement. Green Money comes in two forms: "lazy" and "productive." Lazy green money includes typical bank accounts, CDs, and money markets with minimal upside potential. Productive green money, however, offers fixed rates equivalent to bank accounts based on the current interest rate environment, but with higher upside potential by being linked to an index like the S&P 500. We'll cover these productive tools in a later Chapter 9.

  Green Money is dependable, unlike "at-risk" Red and Yellow Money, which is exposed to market fluctuations but offers growth opportunities. Red money is fully exposed to market upsides and downsides, with the potential to grow or lose value without a safety net.

- **Yellow Money** prioritizes both safety and growth by using market-based tools that have strong upside potential but also have a defined outcome as it relates to downside protection. Although yellow money does involve market risk, it's controlled risk using investment tools that are managed from a loss mitigation perspective. We will die deeper in the yellow money in the next chapter.

- **Red Money** is market-based investments that has zero loss mitigation protection. With red money you're simply at the mercy of market performance being good or bad and there's always that potential of large market losses while being **overexposed** to red money. There's nothing wrong with keeping a portion of your portfolio as red money. You just want to understand the purpose of the money and understand the risk involved. Falling into the trap of being overexposed to red money as you are near or entering retirement could potentially set you up for devastating consequences when we go through the next multi-year-bear market.

Green Money	Red Money	Yellow Money
"Green Money" is safer.	"Red Money" is at risk.	"Yellow Money" is controlled risk.
This money offers a minimum guarantee and it won't go backwards because the market is going backwards.	This is money that can go up or down in value. It may pose a risk if it is not properly managed to serve a specific purpose in a comprehensive plan.	Yellow Money is money that is invested in a way that provides some level of loss mitigation protection.

The fact of the matter is that many people are unaware of their risk exposure. Organizing your assets visually is a crucial way to understand your financial situation. Simply list your assets and assign them a color, working with a Fiduciary Financial Professional for clarity before making any important allocation decisions. This process can reveal the extent of your market risk, as many are surprised to find a significant portion in red money investments due to common misconceptions about market investments.

FOUR MAJOR MYTHS AND MISCONCEPTIONS ABOUT WEALTH MANAGEMENT

In the financial industry, countless myths, misconceptions, and half-truths bombard us daily. This book aims to help you navigate through this noise. By revealing the insider's perspective, you'll understand why these myths persist and who benefits from them. Learning about the motives, loyalties, and persuasive tactics employed by financial influencers will empower you to pursue financial independence more effectively.

MYTH #1: The best way to grow wealth and create income during retirement is to invest in a diversified portfolio of mutual funds: People often view equities for growth and bonds for safety, but both are really Red Money. Bonds encompass various types and risks, including credit, default, and interest rate risks. Traditional 60/40 bond-stock portfolios are perceived as safe, yet bond investments are not immune to losses, especially if interest rates rise, impacting bond values and income streams. For example, in 2022 Intermediate Bond performance ended at -27% for the year. Today's retirees have better options with bond alternatives such as "productive" green money tools that have a contractual guarantee of principal with market linked upside potential that can be used as well as yellow money that is market based but with built in loss mitigation protection.

Speaking of diversification, I would be remiss if I didn't bring up the S&P 500 and the various mutual funds that track it. In 2023, the S&P 500 was up over 24% in a phenomenal year no doubt. So, people believe that investing in a mutual fund that holds those 500 stocks has them, diversified. But in reality, they are not. The reason is because the S&P 500 is a "market capitalization", weighted index. This means that the biggest companies have the biggest impact on their overall performance, whether good or bad. In 2023, 80% of the S&P 500's performance came from just ten stocks.* There were 10 gigantic technology companies that included the so-called "Magnificent Seven" (Apple, Google, Tesla, Meta, Microsoft, Nvidia, Amazon) that make up roughly 30% of the S&P 500. So, it's very deceptive if investors believe they're in a diversified portfolio of 500 stocks. In reality, they're in a portfolio that currently has 30% concentrated in the technology sector, likely a lot more aggressive than they realize. I'm not denying that currently these are some of the top U.S. growth companies. My point is that it is unwise to concentrate so heavily in one sector or industry, especially for retirement income planning.

MYTH #2: When the market crashes, just hang in there, suck it up, and stay for the long haul: We've discussed the common belief that market downturns are just paper losses, but in Chapter 1 we proved why this isn't accurate. Once money leaves your account, you lose the opportunity for compound growth. This is particularly harmful for retirees who can't replenish lost funds, emphasizing the need to minimize risk exposure, especially in retirement.

MYTH #3: Never buy an annuity or cash value your life insurance. Be cautious of anyone who dismisses certain financial tools entirely. Investment tools aren't inherently good or bad; it depends on how they are used. The wrong application of a tool can be harmful to your retirement. Think of financial products as tools in a toolbox—you wouldn't use a hammer to dig a hole or a shovel to pound a nail. Each tool has its purpose, just as certain financial products are better suited for specific needs. When someone criticizes a financial tool broadly, it often means they either don't understand it or can't offer it. A professional

---

* Nasdaq article: "What's Ahead for the 10 Stocks That Have Driven Over 80% of U.S. Market Returns So Far in 2023," published on May 31, 2023.

held to fiduciary standards has a deeper toolbox than most professionals because they are not working for a captive company with proprietary products. Their job is to discover what financial tools can best help you meet your goals. Do you need a saw, a screwdriver, or a hammer to build a strong house? The answer is you need all three.

MYTH #4: The only way to get a reasonable rate of return on your money is to risk money in the stock market. As a retiree facing various risks like market volatility, inflation, and healthcare expenses, you may feel the need to protect your money. However, Wall Street and brokers may urge you to *stay fully invested* in "red" money (stocks, bonds, REIT's) oftentimes to collect fees. They emphasize "buy & hold" to avoid missing out on market gains. But consider another perspective: focus on avoiding losses during retirement, as discussed in Chapter 1.

You don't need to only rely on red money investments to earn good and reasonable returns in retirement. How you organize your assets should align with your goals and risk tolerance, which affect your returns. Based on your preferred risk level, structure your portfolio accordingly. If you're overexposed to market risk with too much red money, consider reallocating adding more yellow and green money. A fiduciary financial professional can help you find the right balance and reallocate your assets as needed.

HOW MUCH OF WHAT COLOR?

The next step is determining the appropriate ratio of Red, Yellow and Green Money for your retirement stage. Relying heavily on Red Money and gambling all assets on the market, regardless of how you feel about the Rule of 100, is extremely risky. Market investments may not reliably generate income, and over-reliance on Red Money can lead to failure, especially when driven by emotional reactions to market fluctuations. This strategy is not only unwise but also stressful for investors banking everything on stocks, ETF's and mutual funds.

A plan that uses too much traditional "Lazy" Green Money tools that avoiding all volatility and can also fail. Why? Investing all your money in CDs, savings accounts, and money markets may provide some income, but it likely won't generate enough growth to keep up with inflation. Additionally, if these are held in a non-retirement account, they generate "ordinary income," which is taxed at a higher rate compared to the more favorable "capital gains" tax treatment. As of this writing, we're experiencing higher historical rates on short-term instruments. For instance, it's not uncommon to find a Money Market account yielding 5%. However, the 12-month percentage change as of March 2024* for medical services is 5.4% and energy is 10.7%. You likely have personal examples of items that have risen in price by more than 5% in the last 12 months. The Federal Reserve recently announced a 50-basis point cut, and has signal more to come. So, we expect to see those favorable yields on short-term CDs and money markets beginning to disappear. If you rely solely on income from traditional "lazy" green money tools and avoid "productive" green money, yellow money, dividend stocks, ETFs, or mutual funds, your portfolio may lack the long-term growth needed to remain healthy. Today, more productive Green Money options with higher upside potential are available, which we will explore in a later chapter. The Rule of 100 can guide you in determining how much of your portfolio should be invested in the market to meet your future needs.

As you age, green money gains significance. While converting red money to yellow and green money is vital, not all of it needs to generate immediate income. Taking a closer look at your money, you will see that you need different amounts at different times.

---

* *www.bls.gov*

Working with a fiduciary retirement income specialist can help you allocate the right amount of money to the appropriate color categories to meet your objectives while maintaining a focus on your risk tolerance.

TYPES OF MONEY: *NEED NOW AND NEED LATER*

"Green Money" is money you'll need for safe growth, income or planned spending within the next 12 to 24 months. After covering your initial retirement income gap, surplus funds can be categorized as Need Now or Need Later money. Need Now money is for emergency funds, planned spending, and income to meet your basic needs and maintain your lifestyle. Your **Need Now Money is your "paycheck" money. Money used for accumulation is Need Later Money**. This is money that you don't need now for income but will need to rely on down the road. You might think of this as your **"playcheck"** money. When the market is doing well, you might carve off a little profit and have a little extra fun! When the market is doing poorly, you still have those reliable paychecks coming in, so you don't have to worry about your core income needs and can hold off on taking any money out of your market-based tools that are likely down. Need Later Money serves as future income, essential for retirement planning. Balancing assets between immediate income and future accumulation is crucial for a strong and financially worry-free retirement.*

OPTIMIZING RISK AND FINDING THE RIGHT BALANCE

Determining the amount of risk that is right for you depends on your specific situation. It starts by examining your financial position. The Rule of 100 is a useful way to begin to deliberate the

---

* *Tom Hegna's book Paychecks and Playchecks*

right amount of risk for you. But remember, it's just a baseline. Use it as a starting point for figuring out where your money should be. If you're a 50-year-old investor, the Rule of 100 suggests that you have 50 percent in "productive" green money and 50 percent red & yellow money. Many 50-year-olds are more risk tolerant, however. There are many reasons why someone might be more risk tolerant, not the least of which is feeling young! Experienced investors, people who feel they need to gamble for a higher return, or people who have met their retirement income goals and are looking for more ways to accumulate wealth are all candidates for investment strategies that incorporate higher levels of risk. In the end, it comes down to your personal tolerance for risk. How much are you willing or can afford to lose?

Consulting with a fiduciary financial professional is often the wisest approach to calculating your risk level. A professional can help determine your risk tolerance by getting to know you, asking you a set of questions and even completing a risk tolerance, questionnaire to determine your comfort level with market risk.

CHAPTER 4 QUICK TIPS //

- Choose a fiduciary retirement income planner with access to the full spectrum of the colors of money offering tools for both growth and protection. As Coach Paul "Bear" Bryant said, "Offense sells tickets, but defense wins championships." In retirement, it's the defense that you apply to your investments that will help you sleep well at night and win the retirement game.

- Beware of brokers using an outdated Rule of 100, exposing all your money to risk. The old model relies solely on stocks and bonds—red money without loss mitigation or any tools with guaranteed principal protection.

- Using the Rule of 100 and a risk tolerance questionnaire is a good starting point to determine how much of your portfolio to allocate to red, yellow, and green money, as well as the amount to categorize as "need-now" and "need-later" funds.

5
YELLOW MONEY:
INVESTMENT STRATEGIES FOR MORE SECURE GROWTH

"Protect the Downside and the Upside Will Take Care of Itself"
– Donald J Trump, 45th President of the United States

Now that you've calculated the Rule of 100, determine how much risk you have and how much you want, and you determine how much "Lazy" Green Money you need to meet your short-term and mid-term cash needs (emergency funds and planned spending over 12-24 months) and "Productive" Green for your core lifestyle to secure your income needs, it's time to look at what you have left. The money you have left after you've calculated your green money needs has the potential of becoming Red Money: stocks, bonds, mutual funds and other investment products that you want deployed into the markets for future security or legacy goals. You now have the luxury of taking a closer second look at your red money to determine how you would like to manage it because your core income needs are now secured.

As you read earlier in the key findings of the DALBAR report, the average investor earns significantly less than the actual performance of their mutual funds. Much of this is due to investor emotions and attempts at market timing, underscoring the substantial risks in managing your red money, which can have a lasting impact on your assets and your ability to create rising income in the future. So, how much of your red money do you invest and in what kinds of investment tools do you use? There are a lot of different directions in which you can take your red money. One thing is for sure: **significant accumulation overtime depends on investing in markets.** Everyone approaches this differently. Without a cohesive strategy, simply accumulating stocks, bonds, real estate, and investment funds may prevent you from benefiting fully from a more organized approach. This can lead to a lack of understanding of your investments, where your money is, and the purpose behind each tool.

Even if you have goals for each part of your portfolio, you may lack a comprehensive plan for your Red Money. This exposes you to more risk than you realize by not properly aligning your assets with your objectives, whether for immediate or future income through a quality dividend income portfolio, growth with loss mitigation, or legacy and tax benefits.

Enter **Yellow money.** Yellow money is money that is invested with *a loss mitigation strategy to help protect the downside.*

After your income needs are met and you have assets that you would like to dedicate to accumulation, there are decisions you need to make about how to invest those assets. You can buy stocks, index funds, mutual funds, bonds—you name it—you can invest in it. However, the difference between Red Money and Yellow

Money is that Yellow Money includes investment tools that have a defined outcome managed from a loss mitigation perspective. There is no money manager guesswork as to when to go to safety to protect the downside and when to stay deployed for upside potential.

Yellow money is still at risk but it is *controlled risk.* We recommend the buffered index note strategy as the primary "Yellow Money" tool for our client family. Despite its long history, many investors are still unaware of its value in a diversified investment portfolio. A buffered index note strategy can be implemented with individual notes from large banks like JP Morgan or UBS. If you use individual notes, ensure you choose a strong financial institution, as the primary risk with this strategy is the issuing bank's credit risk or potential default.

Another way to implement this strategy is by purchasing a basket of notes, such as an exchange-traded fund, which eliminates credit risk. Buffered index note strategy options can vary greatly as it relates to their terms, downside protection and upside potential so it will be important to work with someone who is experienced with this type of loss mitigation tool. But the basic idea is to link your money to an index like the S&P 500 for a specific term (i.e. 12-24 months.). If you liquidate during the "term" you may get back more or less than you put in, based upon how long you have held the note and performance of the S&P 500 or specific index you linked to.

The best practice is to hold the note for the chosen term. Generally, the longer the term, the higher the potential upside or "cap" on S&P 500 performance. As I mentioned earlier, there are many variations of this tool, even ones that will provide 100% downside protection. But let's assume you use a buffered index strategy with a -15% buffer on the S&P 500 and a 14% upside potential or "cap" over 12 months. In this example, on a "gross" performance basis*, if the market falls over the next 12 months but not more than -15%, you will still receive your principal back. However, let's say over that 12-month time. The market drops -20% in that case you would absorb the 5% loss that exceeded the buffer.

The illustration here will help with the concept of how this tool works: If you invest $100,000 in a 12-month note with a -15% buffer, and the market declines over that period, as long as the S&P 500 doesn't drop more than -15%, you'll still have your $100,000 at the end of the term. You lose nothing due to the market fall, while your friends that invested directly in a fund that tracks the S&P 500 would realize a -15% loss in this scenario.

If, after 12 months, the market performs well, you will receive 100% of the S&P 500's positive performance up to that cap of 14%. So, if the S&P 500 gains 20%, your return is capped at 14%. During one of our retirement workshops, an attendee asked, "Eric, how often has the S&P 500 exceeded 14% in the past 20 years?" The answer: "only 6 times." This strategy allows you to capture most of the S&P 500's historical annual performance while limiting your downside. If the market drops -30%, your loss is buffered at -15%, which is a significant advantage over a direct S&P 500 investment… pretty sweet huh?

Gross performance examples do not consider any fees or expense ratios. Caps and terms change each month before funds are actually deployed into the strategy but are then locked in for the term or outcome period chosen.

Loss Mitigation Tool: Buffered Index Strategy

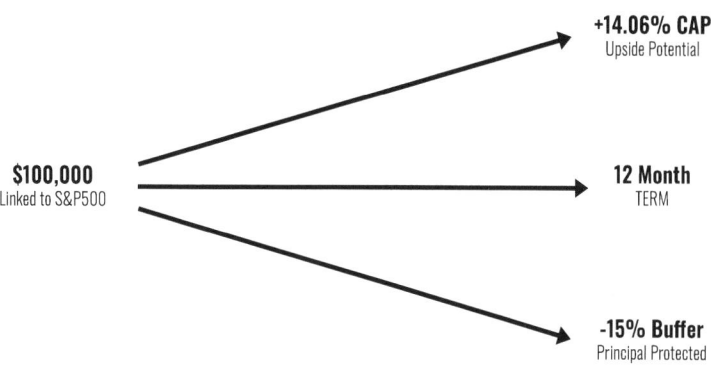

The example above is a hypothetical example and should not be construed the terms of your actual note. Terms change and will be different.

TAKING A CLOSER LOOK AT YELLOW MONEY

*The visual below gives you another hypothetical example of how using a **Yellow Money tool with loss mitigation protection** can provide good upside potential combined with the peace of mind that comes from having downside protection.*

Investor #1 has $100,000 in a "buy & hold" portfolio mirroring the S&P 500, all Red Money. Investing with this strategy of always being in the market gives this investor the opportunity to capture 100 percent of the upside of the market in any given year but without any safety net or strategy to protect their money when the market falls. As a result of this strategy, let's assume the investor loses -15% in the first year but gains 20% in year two. Do the math, and you get a portfolio that is averaging a 2% return and a portfolio balance of $102,000 before any investment fees or expenses have been applied.

Investor #2 uses Yellow Money or a buffered note strategy with a defined outcome or built-in -15% loss mitigation to protect against downside risk. Starting with $100,000 investor

#2 experienced no losses during that -15% market drop. In the second year, despite the cap limiting gains, Investor #2 achieved a 14% return compared to Investor #1's 20% return for a total gain of 14% vs 2%. Are you beginning to see the power of protecting the downside for your retirement funds during the distribution phase?

Investor #1 Buy & Hold $100,000	Investor #2 -15% B.I.N. $100,000
- 15% Loss: $85,000	0% Loss: $100,000
20% Gain: $102,000	14% Gain: $114,000
Total Value UP 2%	**Total Value UP 14%**

Hypothetical example for education purposes only; should not be construed as a guarantee of performance or loss mitigation.
*Gross return does not reflect any potential advisory fees or expense ratios

Imagine you're retired and rely on your investment portfolio for monthly income, supplementing your Social Security and/or pension. Which investor would you rather be Investor #1 or Investor #2? Yeah, it's kind of a *"no brainer"* isn't it?

For those nearing or in retirement, the timing of losses is crucial. As we discussed in an earlier chapter the "retirement red zone" is the 5 to 7 years before retirement, where market losses can severely impact your long-term financial security. A -15% to -20% loss during this period, compounded with potential withdrawals, can severely weaken your portfolio and jeopardize its ability to sustain you. **When building your retirement income plan, implement loss mitigation strategies for your market-based tools.** This will help protect against downturns, provide financial peace of mind ensuring you sleep well during retirement.

TAKING A CLOSER LOOK AT YOUR PORTFOLIO

Think about your investment portfolio. Think specifically of what you would consider your Red Money. Do you know what is there? You may have several different investment products like individual mutual funds, bond accounts, stocks, etc. You may have inherited a stock portfolio from a relative, own a variable annuity, or you may have an account at one of the big brokerage houses. Whether or not you manage your investments yourself, it's likely that you lack a comprehensive strategy with loss mitigation. Unmanaged investments that have no built-in loss mitigation protection are simply "red money"—money 100% at risk in the market.

Harnessing the earning potential of your "red money" requires more than just a collection of stocks and bonds; it needs guided management. A Fiduciary Retirement Income Planner evaluates your full financial picture—risk tolerance, goals, timeline, income needs, legacy plans, tax strategies for retirement accounts, tools for long-term care cost and the proper allocation to the colors of money.

When you meet with an investment professional, you can review all your assets together. Over the past 20-30 years, you may have accumulated various accounts, like a 401(k), IRA, Roth IRA, self-directed stocks, and brokerage accounts. A Fiduciary Retirement Income Planner will assess your current and future risk exposure. They will also help you decide which accounts to use for income generation and which to utilize for long-term growth and future security. We've discussed risk extensively. One crucial question to ask yourself is, "Do I know how much market risk I am currently exposed to?" **If we face another multiyear, bear market like the Great Recession, where the market lost**

over 50% peak to trough do you know how far your portfolio could fall?

If you don't, when would be the best time to find out—before or after it happens? Another no-brainer, right? If you're working with someone you consider a trusted financial professional, schedule an appointment with them as soon as possible and ask these questions:

1. If we face another 2008-like market or a Great Recession, what is our loss mitigation plan?
2. If we face another 2008-like market or Great Recession and I leave my portfolio as recommended, by what percentage can I expect it to fall by?

Now, after posing those two questions you get a deer-in-the-headlight stare or the same old Wall Street rhetoric like, "the market's down, but it's just a paper loss. If you sell now, you'll never get your money back, and besides, you're in it for the long haul," guess what you have just discovered? That you are working with a broker and not a retirement income planning specialist. We have all heard that generic advice and it can be dangerous for someone in or nearing retirement. As I've previously mentioned there is nothing wrong with brokers. They can be effective during the wealth accumulation phase. You just need to know who you're working with during this season of your financial life. The person or persons who may have helped you get TO retirement may or may not be the person or person to help you get THROUGH retirement successfully!

You are in a season of life with the money you have accumulated means more to you now than has ever met in your entire lifetime. It's essential to work with a fiduciary retirement income planning specialist who possesses a distinct set of skills and disciplines necessary for this stage of your financial life.

AVOIDING EMOTIONAL INVESTING

There's no way around it; people get emotional about their money. And for good reasons. You've spent your life working for it, exchanging your time and talent for it, and making decisions about how to invest it, save it, and make it grow. The maintenance of your lifestyle and your plans for retirement all depend on it. The best investment strategies, however, don't rely on emotions.

A well-managed investment account meets your objectives for income, growth, risk exposure, legacy and the lifetime tax mitigation goals you have for your qualified retirement accounts, not in individualized or piecemeal ways.

For example, if you want your portfolio to be used for income, which would call for lower risk and less upside potential , your professional will screen for and build you a portfolio for sustainable and increasing dividend yield and sector diversification. A professional will create a portfolio that reflects your investment desires. If some of the current assets you own complement the strategies that your professional recommends, those will likely stay in your portfolio.

Screening your assets removes emotions from the equation. It also removes attachment to underperforming or overly risky investments. Fiduciary Retirement Income Planners aren't married to particular stocks, ETF's or mutual funds for any reason. They go by the numbers and see your portfolio through a lens shaped by your retirement goals. A fiduciary professional will understand your wants and needs and will create an investment strategy that takes your life events and future plans into account. It's a thoughtful approach, and it allows you to tap into the tools and resources of a professional who has built a career around successful investing.

Building a portfolio based on your goals and risk tolerance, using the "colors of money" and implementing loss mitigation, helps remove emotions from investing. This approach allows you to stay on the course with confidence during market volatility. A fiduciary financial professional doesn't focus on where the market will be in a month or a year. Historically, the stock market has trended upward since the early 20th century, despite events like the Great Depression, Great Recession (2007-2009) and the Covid Pandemic. We have seen the markets continue to recover and push forward during these times. The S&P 500, after losing 57% from October 15th, 2007, to March 9th 2009, not only recovered but grew over 748%* as of October 1, 2024. Emotional investing leads to buying high and selling low, which is costly. While you can't afford to lose the money you'll need in the near term, your long-term investments should be positioned for growth and able to endure some market drawdowns over time.

One of the best ways to avoid emotional investing is by creating an appropriate portfolio based on your goals and risk tolerance, upfront. And ensure you incorporate all three "colors" of money:

1. **"Productive" Green Money:** Retirement products that protect against market downturns by offering a guaranteed principal or lifetime income, effectively creating a personal pension.

2. **Red Money:** Investments that offer long-term growth potential and dividend income strategies but lack principal protection.

3. **Yellow Money:** Investment that provides loss mitigation protection while at the same time offering strong upside potential as well.

Working with a professional will help you determine how much risk you should take, how to balance your assets so they will meet

---

* *Officialdata.org*

your goals and how to plan for the big-ticket items, like health care expenses, that may be in your future. Yes, Yellow Money is exposed to risk, but it is controlled risk, and by working with a fiduciary retirement professional, you can manage that risk with a defined outcomes with yellow money.

SAVE TIME; ENJOY RETIREMENT

A Fiduciary Retirement Income Planning Specialist has expertise in managing money wisely. Relying on them, along with using all the colors of money for your investment portfolio, alleviates the stress, time commitment, and cost of managing your assets yourself. This approach allows you to enjoy retirement without the daily concern of asset allocation decisions, so you can focus on living your life instead of worrying about buying and selling stocks or chasing mutual funds or ETF's.

CHAPTER 5 QUICK TIPS //

- Converting some red money to yellow money offers strong upside potential with downside protection, helping guard against downturns and providing peace of mind in retirement.

- Visit: thefinancialhq.com/ets to learn your color of money risk score. This is one of the first steps on the road to retirement.

- To learn more about the current yellow money options available to you and how it may enhance your existing portfolio, call 770-904-1978 or email info@etswealth.com.

6
A GAME PLAN FOR RISING INCOME

"It's not how much money you make, but how much money you keep, how hard it works for you, and how many generations you keep it for."
— Robert Kiyosaki

A successful retirement income plan must include a strategy to generate rising income over time to combat inflation, taxes, to build wealth for future security, and maintain your lifestyle. As of this writing, inflation has been a significant concern for several years. According to the U.S. Bureau of Labor Statistics (BLS), the Consumer Price Index (CPI) inflation rate peaked at 9.1% in June 2022 and has since decreased to around 3.7% as of August 2023. However, many goods and services within the index still reflect higher prices, for example, used vehicles and dining out are above

5% and shelter is still up 7.2% year over year. Inflation remains a major concern for retirees on fixed incomes, underscoring the need for a comprehensive retirement income plan that includes tools to provide rising income throughout retirement.

The bottom line is that keeping pace with, or outpacing inflation is crucial, especially for retirees. As prices rise, each dollar's value decreases, meaning the same amount of money buys less and less. **Like termites silently eating away at the foundation of a house**, inflation gradually weakens the purchasing power of your money, often unnoticed until it's too late and you fall so far behind that it is extremely difficult to catch up and regain the lifestyle you once enjoyed.

SO, WHAT CAUSES INFLATION?

Inflation can be caused by a variety of factors, and oftentimes it's a combination of factors that drives prices up. According to Investopedia, here are just a few of the most common factors that can cause inflation:

1. **Demand-Pull Inflation:** This occurs when the demand for goods and services exceeds their supply. When people have more money, they tend to spend more. If the production of goods and services doesn't keep up with this increased demand, prices will rise.

2. **Built-In Inflation**: Sometimes referred to as wage-price inflation, this occurs when businesses increase wages to keep up with the rising cost of living, and then pass these higher labor costs onto consumers in the form of higher prices. This can create a cycle where wages and prices continuously push each other higher.

3. **Monetary Expansion:** When a government increases the money supply by printing more money or through other means, it can lead to inflation if the amount of goods and

services in the economy doesn't increase at the same rate. More money in circulation can decrease the value of the currency, leading to higher prices for goods and services.

INFLATION FIGHTING SOLUTIONS:

Historically, several investment tools have been effective in helping offset inflation:

1. **Stocks/Equities:** Stocks have historically provided returns that outpaced inflation over the long term. Growth stocks tend to perform well in inflationary environments.

2. **Real Estate:** Real estate often serves as a hedge against inflation because property values and rental income tend to rise with inflation. This is especially true for **income-generating properties**, where rents can be adjusted for inflation.

3. **Commodities**: Commodities like gold, oil, and agricultural products typically rise in value during inflation. Gold, especially, is considered a safe-haven asset and has long been used as a hedge against inflation.

4. **Treasury Inflation-Protected Securities** (TIPS) and **Inflation-Linked Bonds:** TIPS are government bonds designed to protect against inflation. Their principal value adjusts (up and down) with the Consumer Price Index (CPI), ensuring your investment retains its real value.

5. **Dividend-Paying Stocks:** Stocks with a long-term history of not only paying dividends but increasing them over time can also serve as an excellent hedge against inflation.

THE POWER AND POTENTIAL OF A HIGH-QUALITY DIVIDEND INCOME PORTFOLIO

Each of the above tools has unique benefits and risks, and their effectiveness can vary depending on the specific inflationary environment. However, the tool I want to focus on now is a high-quality portfolio of dividend income stocks. **A well-constructed dividend income portfolio not only generates income but also has the potential for increasing income throughout retirement.**

ONE SOLID SOLUTION TO CONSIDER...

The **"ETS Diversified Income Portfolio."** We continually analyze what we believe to be the best dividend income paying stocks to build and manage our portfolio internally. Our current portfolio includes 20 high quality, strong yielding, blue chip stocks with 5 complementary mutual funds and/or ETFs for additional portfolio diversification. There are numerous financial metrics that we screen for and below are a few of the key ones:

1. **Years of Consecutive Dividend Increases:** our current portfolio of stocks has not only paid dividends but has increased them from anywhere between 5 to 55 years

2. **Diversification by Both Sector and Industry:** Currently this portfolio is diversified among 10 different sectors and 9 separate industries.

3. **Dividend Yield:** As of August 29, 2024, the current gross yield for "The ETS Diversified Income" portfolio is just over 6.7%. Inexperienced investors can be hurt by chasing high yields (7.5%+). If a yield seems too good to be true, it is likely. Proceed with caution when buying such high-yield stocks.

4. **Tax Efficiency:** The majority of the dividends generated from our portfolio are "qualified dividends," meaning

that the bulk of the income generated from a non-IRA account, receive preferable, capital gains tax treatment vs. ordinary income treatment.

5. **Conservative payout ratios:** the "dividend payout ratio" is the percentage of profits that the company pays out in dividends. The Motley Fool suggests that a payout ratio above 80% might be risky, especially if the company's earnings are volatile. A payout ratio over 100% is concerning, as it means the company pays more in dividends than it earns, relying on debt or reserves which is obviously unsustainable long-term and risk's a future dividend cut. The payout ratios in our **"ETS Diversified Income"** portfolio range from 43% to 74%, with the company at 74% increasing dividends for 55 consecutive years.

In retirement, a solid dividend income portfolio can also support your legacy goals. Since you are generating income from dividends rather than selling shares, the share prices could grow over time leaving a bigger legacy for your beneficiaries. When they inherit the shares in a non-retirement account under current tax law, they receive the value of those funds without tax as they would receive a step up in cost basis and also could continue receiving the dividends that could provide lifetime income for your heirs.

Remember dividends are not guaranteed so it is important to create a solid portfolio with quality positions, monitored very closely, and make changes when necessary, especially when dividend cuts do occur.

CHAPTER 6 QUICK TIPS //

- By converting some of your Red Money previously earmarked for growth into a dividend income portfolio, you have the potential to create rising income throughout your retirement.
- Chasing high yields can be tempting, but they often come with significant risk.
- Focus on companies with strong financials, a history of dividend growth, and reasonable payout ratios
- To learn more about the **"ETS Diversified Income"** portfolio and how it may enhance your existing portfolio, call 770-904-1978 or email info@etswealth.com.

7
GETTING THE MOST OUT OF SOCIAL SECURITY

*Social Security is not an entitlement, it is your money!
You paid into the system all of your working life. Make
sure the politicians never forget that fact!*

In 2024 an average of almost 68 million Americans per month will receive a Social Security benefit totaling about $1.5 trillion in benefits paid during the year!*

One kind of Green Money that most Americans rely on as a foundation for their retirement income is Social Security. As a first step in creating your income plan review your Social Security filing options with a financial professional to determine that

---

* http://www.ssa.gov/pressoffice/basicfact.htm

you are making the proper filing choices to fit your needs and maximize your benefits.

> » *Nelly had dedicated nearly her entire adult life to full-time work, eagerly anticipating retirement with her husband, children, and grandchildren. At 62, she eagerly tapped into her Social Security benefits, marking a significant new chapter in her life. A few years into retirement, while organizing papers in her home office, Nelly stumbled upon an old Social Security statement.*
>
> *Reflecting on the statement, Nelly realized she might have made a premature decision. Having saved adequately, she could have afforded to delay her benefits and secure a higher monthly payout. When she was in the process of retiring, there were so many other decisions to make and filing for Social Security had seemed straightforward at the time. Now, she considered contacting the Social Security Administration to explore the possibility of increasing her benefits to a larger amount.*

Unfortunately, she will not be able to increase her amount. Once you begin to take Social Security, you have one year to determine if you may have made a mistake. If so, you must pay all the money back and get "do-over."

Here are some facts that illustrate how Americans currently use Social Security:

- Nearly 90% of Americans age 65 and older receive Social Security benefits.*
- Social Security represents about 30% of the income of people over age 65.*

---

* http://www.ssa.gov/pressoffice/basicfact.htm

- Claiming Social Security benefits at the wrong time can significantly reduce your monthly lifetime benefits.*
- In January 2024, the average monthly Social Security benefit was $1,907 and *the maximum benefit equaled $3,822.***

Social Security is a complex program with many nuances, and when it's time to claim benefits, you'll face numerous options. It's a vast system that experts spend their entire careers mastering, but you don't need to know every detail to make the right choices. A fiduciary retirement income specialist can guide you in making the best decisions for you and your family. Understanding the optimal strategies for claiming Social Security can enhance your retirement plan. It's important to invest time in developing a strategy to maximize these benefits and integrate them into your overall retirement plan. While you can't control how much you contribute or how it's managed, you do have control over when and how you file for benefits. The real question that you need to answer is, "When should I start taking Social Security?"

While you can begin collecting benefits as early as age 62, the amount you receive as a monthly benefit will be less than it would be if you wait until you reach what is called your "Full Retirement Age" (FRA). It is important to note that if you file for your Social Security benefit before your FRA, **the reduction to your monthly benefit will remain in place for the rest of your life.** You can also delay receiving benefits up to age 70, in which case your benefits will be higher than your FRA amount for the rest of your life.

At FRA, 100 percent of what is called your Primary Insurance Amount (PIA) is available as a monthly benefit.

---

* https://www.ssa.gov/planners/retire/retirechart.html

** https://www.ssa.gov/news/press/factsheets/colafacts2024.html

At age 62, your Social Security retirement benefits are available. For each month you take benefits prior to your FRA, however, the monthly amount of your benefit is reduced. ***This reduction stays in place for the rest of your life.***

At age 70, your monthly benefit reaches its maximum. After you turn age 70, your monthly benefit will no longer increase.*

Year of Birth	Full Retirement Age
1943-1954	66
1955	66 and 2 months
1956	66 and 4 months
1957	66 and 6 months
1958	66 and 8 months
1959	66 and 10 months
1960 or later	age 67**

ROLLING UP YOUR SOCIAL SECURITY

Your Social Security income "rolls up" or increases by 8% a year <u>each year</u> you wait to claim it up to age 70. For many, creating the right Social Security strategy is crucial to enhancing their retirement, potentially impacting their benefits by tens of thousands of dollars over a lifetime.

Deciding NOW or LATER: Following this logic, it seems to make sense to delay starting your Social Security benefits. However, the decision isn't always straightforward. Not everyone can afford to wait; many rely on these benefits from the start of their retirement. Some need the income immediately, while others, facing health issues, may not see the value in waiting until full retirement age for themselves or their families. Additionally, many who claim benefits early at age 62 may simply be misinformed

---

* *https://www.ssa.gov/news/press/basicfact.html*
** *http://www.ssa.gov/OACT/progdata/nra.html*

about Social Security, making decisions based on rumors and emotions rather than facts.

File Immediately if You:
- Find your job is unbearable and you need cash flow.
- Are not interested in "front loading" your retirement income
- Are not healthy and need a reliable source of income.

Consider Delaying Your Benefit if You:
- Have longevity and want to maximize your retirement income in later years.
- Want to increase retirement benefits for your spouse.
- Are still working and like it.

Let's take a look at an example that shows the impact of working with a financial professional to optimize Social Security benefits:

> » *George and Monica Haymaker, a typical American couple, have worked hard and saved when possible. George is 60, and Monica is 56. During a meeting with a financial professional, they logged onto the Social Security website to check their PIAs—$1,900 for George and $900 for Monica. If the Haymakers start taking Social Security benefits at age 62, they will receive an estimated $568,600 in lifetime benefits, averaging about $28,400 per year—much lower than they're accustomed to. However, if they wait until their full retirement age (FRA), their lifetime benefits would increase to an estimated $609,000, providing them with $34,200 annually. After analyzing their needs and using specialized software, the financial professional found that the optimal filing strategy could boost their lifetime benefits to $649,000. By following these recommendations, the Haymakers increased*

their potential profits by as much as $80,000. This example shows how crucial it is to analyze your Social Security filing options. For the Haymakers, maximizing their benefits made a significant difference, and such benefit increases are not uncommon.

MAXIMIZING YOUR LIFETIME BENEFIT

As discussed, calculating how to maximize **benefits for the life expectancy that you would like to use for planning purposes** is more important than simply waiting until age 70 for your maximum **monthly benefit amount.** It's about getting the most income during your lifetime. Professional benefit maximization software can target the year and month that it is most beneficial for you to file based on your life expectancy assumptions.

The three common ages associated with retirement benefits are 62 (Earliest Eligible Age), 66 (Full Retirement Age), and 70 (age for maximum monthly benefit). However, none of these typically offer the maximum lifetime benefit. Remember, delaying your claim increases each payment, but you receive fewer checks overall. While you can't predict your exact lifespan, you are likely to have a better understanding of your life expectancy than the Social Security Administration's actuaries, who rely on averages and cannot factor in your individual and family history. A financial professional can work with you to better understand your individual variables and help you calculate the optimal time for you to start benefits, maximizing your lifetime potential—a service not provided by the Social Security Administration.

Types of Social Security Benefits: Although not a complete list of benefit types here are a few of the most common:

- **Retired Worker Benefit.** *This is the most recognized Social Security benefit, based on your earnings and the contributions you've made throughout your career.*

- ***Spousal Benefit:*** *Available to the spouse of someone eligible for Retired Worker Benefits.*

- ***Survivorship Benefit:*** *Allows a surviving spouse to receive the larger of the two benefit amounts when one spouse passes away.*

THE DIVORCE FACTOR

How does a divorced spouse qualify for benefits? If you have gone through a divorce, it might affect the retirement benefit to which you are entitled.

In general, a person can receive benefits as a divorced spouse on a former spouse's Social Security record so long as the following conditions are met:
- the marriage lasted at least 10 years; and
- the person filing for divorce benefits is at least age 62, unmarried, and not entitled to a higher Social Security benefit on his or her own record.*

Filing for Social Security involves navigating numerous options, strategies, and benefits, making it far more complex than merely submitting paperwork. While understanding all your options is essential, it isn't sufficient for making optimal decisions. You could exhaust yourself trying to determine the best choices and still doubt your decisions, or you could consult a financial professional. Using specialized software your fiduciary can generate a "Social Security Maximization Report". With this report a fiduciary professional can account for all the variables in your situation and provide a detailed analysis to help ensure you make an informed decision saving you a tremendous amount of time and complex math.

---

* *http://www.ssa.gov/retire2/yourdivspouse.htm*

The Maximization Report generated by your financial professional is an invaluable tool for understanding how and when to file for your Social Security benefit. This customized report will not only outline all available options but will also explain the financial implications of each. It provides precise recommendations on the optimal aged down to the month and year—to trigger benefits, and how to apply. Additionally, the report includes timely advice on other important actions, such as when to apply for Medicare or take Required Minimum Distributions from your qualified plans. With this report, there's no need to guess or struggle to determine the best times to take action—it clearly presents everything in straightforward terms.

CHAPTER 7 QUICK TIPS //

- Social Security is not only one of the best annuities available, but it is also one of your largest retirement assets. Be smart: before deciding to activate your Social Security benefit, request a Social Security Maximization report from your financial professional. You only get one chance to get it right!

- When it's time to file for benefits, consider filing online. We've found that the staff who respond to calls tend to be savvier than those at the front lines in the administration's office.

- Call 770-904-1974 to find out how you can receive your personalized Social Security Maximization Report.

8
CREATING A SOLID INCOME PLAN

"If your Outgo exceeds your Income, then Upkeep will be your Downfall."
– Attributed to the 20th century philosopher William Earl

Take a moment to think about your income goals:
- What is your lifestyle today?
- Would you like to maintain it or increase it initially in retirement?
- What do you really *need* to live on when you retire?
- How much of your retirement income would you like to have coming in as a **"Sure Thing"** (i.e. Guaranteed). And how much would you be OK with coming from market-based tools defined as a **"Maybe"**?
- Is part-time work in retirement part of your plan?

Some people will have the luxury of maintaining or improving their lifestyle, while others may have to make decisions about what they need versus what they want during their retirement

But everyone, regardless of their income needs, can benefit from having a written plan.

THE IMPORTANCE OF A WRITTEN INCOME PLAN?

I've always said, "Make your plan and work your plan." Just like armies have battle plans and builders have blueprints, you also need a Retirement Income Plan. To achieve a successful, happy and financially worry-free retirement it is necessary to create a retirement vision and a written retirement income plan to make it a reality. This is not optional!

Are you currently working with a trusted broker or financial advisor? Do you have a comprehensive written income plan that ensures you never run out of money and addresses all five key areas (The Five Roadblocks) for a successful, happy, and financially worry-free retirement?

If your answer is "no," then you may miss out on achieving what we call "The Priorities" for our "Client Family Members". And what are "The Priorities"? It's the peace of mind that comes from knowing you'll never again worry about a market crash like 2008 wiping out your savings, lowering your standard of living in retirement, or outliving your income. If these priorities are important to you, but you don't have a comprehensive written retirement income plan, my question is: "Why not?"

You are in a season of life where the money that you've accumulated means more to you now than it has ever meant in your lifetime. You should have a comprehensive written income plan, especially if you're working with a "trusted financial advisor."

Well, there could be a couple of reasons why you might not have a written income plan:

- You might be able to do it yourselfer and manage money for your own account, enjoy it, and do a great job at it. You might have the skill set and the ability to create that comprehensive retirement income plan addressing the "The Five Roadblocks" to a successful retirement, but you just haven't gotten around to it. Here's a recommendation: take a weekend to make the plan and work on the plan.

- It might be that you're working with a "broker" versus a Retirement Income Planning Specialist. Again, there is nothing wrong with brokers, especially if you're in the accumulation phase. But the distribution phase of your life requires an entirely different skill set and approach.

Here's an example of what I mean. When I was a baby, my mother used to take me to a pediatrician. As I got older, I went to a general practitioner, then an internist. Now, I understand, some people will actually go to specialists like cardiologists, pulmonologists, etc. In this season of your life, preparing for retirement, you need to be working with a fiduciary advisory firm that specializes in retirement income planning. You don't need a general practitioner or someone who focuses on an area that you've outgrown. Retirement is a one-act play, if you get it right, you'll enjoy many years of a comfortable retirement. If you get it wrong, you run a much greater risk of running out of money before you run out of life so there is a lot at stake here.

WHAT ARE THE FIVE ROADBLOCKS?

These roadblocks are discovered by asking yourself a few important questions where you must have the correct answers to not only to get TO retirement as well as THROUGH retirement successfully.

1. **What's my monthly spendable** (after-tax) **income that I want, and have I mapped that out for the rest of my/our life expectancy for planning purposes?**

2. **How do I take that monthly income figure and create a rising income stream throughout my retirement lifetime to offset taxes, inflation, and to build wealth for future security such as long-term care costs or legacy goals?**

3. **If married, how will we offset lost income for the surviving spouse when one Social Security benefit is lost, and a potential reduction in pension income as well?**

4. **How will I create a "Loss Mitigation Plan" to protect the downside of my "Red Money" accounts or market-based tools because I don't have time to make up for large losses in the stock and bond markets?**

5. **What's my game plan to minimize taxes over my retirement lifetime?**

Having a comprehensive written plan that includes the correct answers to these five essential questions is important, but it's even more vital to implement the right strategies to address them to ensure a happy and financially worry-free retirement journey.

HOW MUCH AND WHAT KIND?

Every retirement financial strategy must prioritize supporting your intended lifestyle with core income for day-to-day needs. The moment your working income ceases and you start living off the money you've set aside for retirement, you have entered the distribution phase of your financial life. So, while you were climbing the mountain of retirement working, saving and investing, you were in the accumulation phase, and you had time on your side. Because of that you could take a couple of 2008's or a couple great recessions and still be OK. Just like climbing Mount Everest the most dangerous part is not going up the mountain. More people lose their lives, coming down the mountain, than going up!

As you move into the distribution phase of your life, coming down the mountain of retirement investment and allocation strategies change dramatically. Now it's no longer about accumulation. It's about distribution and protecting your asset base from large market losses, unnecessary taxes and penalties, long-term care expenses. You simply cannot follow the same strategies that served you well in the accumulation phase of your life. This includes things such as dollar cost averaging which is taking a certain percentage of your income and allocating it to your investments and 401(k), regardless of if the market is up or down. If you take the same approach with withdrawing a specific percentage, such as 4% from your investments regardless of market volatility that could potentially not only kill your lifestyle, but due to the sequence of returns because you too completely run out of money!

Satisfying that need for daily income entails first knowing *how much you need* and *when you will need it.*

How Much Money Do You Need? Obviously, determining your income needs is key. While it varies, a general rule suggests retirees should aim for 70-80% of pre-retirement income. But it's important to think of retirement in three phases: the first phase or season of retirement, which for some could last a decade-plus, is what we call your "Go-Go Years". In this season, you have health and energy, likely doing more expensive travel, recreation, and activities than in the following two phases of retirement called the "Slow Go" and then the "No Go" years, where activity decreases.

Matching income needs with suitable investment strategies during each season is important to say the least.

It's vital to work with an independent fiduciary investment firm which has access to a wide range of investment tools instead of the firms that promote limited options. For instance, during the "No Go" years, having tools in your portfolio that can leverage funds for long-term care or home healthcare expenses is crucial, rather than relying solely on personal savings especially if legacy planning is an important goal of yours.

Most people are familiar with the typical investment strategies for generating interest or dividend income (CDs, bonds, dividend pay stocks, mutual funds EFT's and real estate investment trust). However, that's not where you should begin.

STEP ONE: "SURE THING OR "MAYBE?: Before allocating income to different investment tools, ask yourself: How much of my core lifestyle income do I want from "Sure Things" or guaranteed sources, like a paycheck or pension, vs. how much am I comfortable with coming from "Maybes" or non-guaranteed sources, like mutual funds or dividend stocks, which can fluctuate and affect lifestyle during market downturns? There's no right or wrong answer to that question however we find that most pre-retirees and retirees prefer having at least 50-60% of their core lifetime income from "Sure Things" like Social Security or pensions offered by their employer or through income annuities if they're not lucky enough to have a pension one through their employer. Having a good portion of your total income coming from "Sure Things" or lifetime guaranteed sources provides invaluable peace of mind.

STEP TWO: CONSIDER YOUR TIMING: For example, if during your go-go years, you would like to have higher income for the first 10 years, opt for a tool that fits; for lifetime income, choose one that's guaranteed to be there and won't deplete. Factor in healthcare, emergencies, and other expenses as well to maximize your overall financial peace of mind during retirement. A Fiduciary Investment Advisor can tailor a comprehensive holistic income plan to your needs. **At our firm, we simply called this the "ETS Retire Ready Plan."**

As we discussed earlier in Chapter 1, one of the most important things you need to do as you create an income plan is to take care to avoid too much exposure to risk. You can start by meeting with a Fiduciary Investment Advisor to organize your assets. Get your Green, Yellow and Red Money in order and balance to meet your needs. If the market goes down -18% this afternoon, you don't want that to come out of what you're relying on for next year's income. **For married couples, it is crucial to strengthen their income plan by addressing how to replace any income lost due to unexpected life events.**

Social Security is a lifelong benefit, but it ends when a person dies. Also, it is no secret that Social Security is underfunded. **In fact, as of November 8, 2023, according to the American Academy of actuaries if Congress does not act by 2034, Social Security may be faced with an automatic 20% benefit cut for current recipients.** Keep this in mind for your income planning to mitigate potential loss of Social Security income in the future.

> » *Robert and Stephanie were high school sweethearts. They did everything together, went to the prom, got married, started a career, and had a family. After the kids were off to college and starting their own lives, Robert and Stephanie paid off the house and retired together at the age of 66.*
>
> *They felt pretty good about their financial future. Lee received a pension from his job that kicked in at the age of 67 in the amount of $36,000 a year. He also had $24,000*

a year coming to him from Social Security benefits. Ann's job did not give her a pension, but she had some money in a 401(k)-plan invested in the stock market, and she received $15,000 a year from Social Security benefits. They wanted to know how to best utilize Ann's investment money, so they talk with a fiduciary financial professional who specialized in income planning. What he showed them really opened their eyes!

First, the professional explained that if Robert died at age 70, Stephanie would not only lose her husband but also half of his pension and one Social Security benefit, reducing her income from $75,000 to $42,000 a year! If she needed long-term care, she couldn't afford the average annual cost of $100,375 for a nursing home in Georgia.* Even if she remained healthy and lived until 85, Stephanie would still miss out on $495,000 in income (her Social Security and ½ of Robert's pension for 15yrs). Realizing that women often outlive men, Stephanie knew she would likely face the similar monthly expenses, plus additional costs like hiring someone to mow the lawn. None of this sounded appealing to Stephanie. Using his "Income for Life" software, their financial professional calculated and advised Stephanie on how to invest her 401(k) funds to secure an additional $40,000 a year in guaranteed income for both of their lifetimes. This retirement income vehicle would be completely protected from market risk. If they never needed to turn on the additional income stream, the money would continue to grow and pass on to their children.

---

* Annual cost of care survey conducted by Carescout,site accessed 03/15/2024

CREATING A SOLID INCOME PLAN

> *Robert and Stephanie left that meeting with a written income plan and smiles on their faces. They no longer had to worry about market risk, inflation and the risk of unexpected events.*

Some retirees like Robert and Stephanie rely on pension income that may cease with the death of a spouse unless provisions are made. Similarly, Social Security, another type of defined-benefit plan, ends upon a person's death, though spousal benefits allow for the selection of the higher of two benefit amounts. **Consequently, the surviving spouse will receive only one check instead of two.** Plus, losing additional pension income on top of Social Security could result in a severe lifetime monthly pay cut. If married, have you considered how a potential lost income could affect the surviving spouse's lifestyle? Would you even be able to continue to meet your core expenses?

In our story above, Robert and Stephanie used a popular annuity tool to create their very own personal pension. These unique tools offer an income stream for you and your spouse, access to cash value, and benefits to your heirs upon your passing. Consult your financial advisor about creating a written income plan that guarantees lifetime payments for you and your spouse. In addition, create a plan to offset any lost income for the surviving spouse. Read on to learn how to get the most out of one of your most important Green Money income sources, your Social Security benefits.

CHAPTER 8 QUICK TIPS //

- Armies have battle plans, builders have blueprints, and Fiduciary Retirement Income Planning Specialists have written income plans and the tools to implement your plan. Don't skip this step. Get a plan, anticipate the obstacles, and avoid the pull of the crowd. My mom always said: "Following the crowd leads nowhere"!

- Annuities are like doctors, there are both good and bad ones out there. By doing your due diligence and finding out where the good ones are, you'll have a much better chance of maintaining both good physical and financial health!

9
HOW TO CREATE CASH FLOW FOR LIFE

In retirement, financial peace of mind comes not from a finite pile of money, but from guaranteed cash flow—lifetime paychecks!

The moment you retire and begin living off your retirement savings you have officially transitioned from the accumulation to the distribution phase of your financial life. After years of earning paychecks from your employer, you now rely on your own assets for income.

If your monthly Social Security check and your other supplemental income leave a shortfall in your *desired* income, how are you going to fix it? This shortfall is called the **Income Gap,** and it must be filled in order to meet your lifestyle goals and enjoy a financially happy and worry-free retirement. You will want to fill that income gap with the least amount of your asset base as possible so you get the most out of the rest of your assets. This includes allocating funds for future security by creating a strategy for rising income, tax shifting in order to mitigate taxes throughout your retirement lifetime, building wealth for medical expenses such as long-term care and meeting your legacy planning goals as well.

As you build your income plan, make sure that you have a minimum of two streams of income "paychecks." These are tools that are guaranteed such as Social Security, Pension Annuity Income, and US Treasuries. These types of tools will provide what we call a "Sure Thing" as it relates to income streams.

And you also want to make sure that you are building in some "playchecks" as well. These will typically be your market-based tools like mutual funds, ETF's and dividend income portfolios that are exposed to market risk. We could even throw in buffered index strategies into this category as well, even though they will provide some level of loss mitigation protection against the S&P 500. All of these types of tools are what are referred to as a "Maybe." There is no guarantee the income projected will be provided as it would be with "Sure Thing" income.

Paychecks and sure things: If you could have the option to contribute more money toward Social Security to secure more guaranteed income, it would be a great way to create a Green Money asset that would enhance your retirement. Since that option isn't available, you may seek an investment tool that is similar to Social Security that provides you with guaranteed lifetime income for not only you but if married, for your spouse as well.

In retirement, financial peace of mind comes not from a large but pile of money, but from guaranteed cash flow—a lifetime paycheck! Adding this element to your portfolio ensures a secure income, allowing you to rest easily without fearing a financial downturn that could deplete this vital part of your nest egg.

THE "A" WORD!

In the past, people depended on traditional pensions backed by insurance companies for steady income. Today, the majority of retirees must create their own income streams, but they can still depend on insurance companies to establish personal pensions for their core income needs. This is possible through personal pension annuities. The "A" Word…annuity" conjures up all kinds of mixed emotions depending on what someone has heard or experienced with this type of tool, but the main thing I want you to understand about annuities is that they are kind of like ice cream- - they come in different flavors. And they're similar to doctors in the sense that there are some doctors you would not want to touch with a 10-foot pole. However, there are some doctors that you would recommend to your best friend and keep them for life. It's the same with annuities. There are good ones and bad ones out there. You just need to know what you're looking for and what to stay away from.

In years past, the old kind of pension annuities were called SPIAs or single, premium, immediate annuities. These kinds of annuities got a bad reputation because they had no access to cash value, and some did not even have a death benefit. So, if you put $100,000 in a old SPIA pension annuity, you are simply trading that lump sum for a lifetime payment. Assume you are receiving $7,000 of yearly guaranteed income for your hundred thousand dollars, and you died after your first payment was received. In many cases with this old type of income tool, the insurance company would keep the remainder of $100,000! Obviously, a great deal for the insurance company who issued the annuity, but certainly not a good deal for the consumer!

So as better and much more consumer-friendly products developed over time they became a much more viable and useful tool in a comprehensive retirement income plan. These newer types of annuities give you a place to put your money where you can turn on an income stream for yourself or your spouse, have access to the cash value and when you pass away, any amount left in the account goes to your beneficiaries.

That is a huge improvement in product design.

There are three primary types of annuities, and not all of them are Green Money tools, which often creates confusion. Here is what you need to know before you order an annuity to satisfy your guaranteed income appetite:

The Traditional Fixed Annuity: A fixed annuity will pay you out interest income based on a guaranteed fixed rate of return similar to a CD. At the writing of this edition interest rates are at historically high levels with the fed funds rate between 5.25% to 5.50%, so we're enjoying higher rates on short-term fixed instruments. Today we're seeing anywhere between 5.10% to 5.6% tax deferred interest depending on the term you choose. This is a safe, Green Money investment. You are guaranteed a set return for the chosen term, with your principal protected by the insurance company's claims-paying ability, so it's important to choose financially strong, reliable insurers.

The Variable Annuity: As the name suggests, variable annuities vary with the market and are a Red Money investment. They do NOT offer a guarantee of your principal but rather offer direct participation in the stock market.

Because variable annuities are invested in mutual funds, there are management fees assessed for each fund in addition to the other expense fees, making the variable annuity one of the more expensive investments that you can own. Here is what financial advisor, author, and television host Suze Orman has to say about variable annuities on page 504 of her book "The Road to Wealth": "For many reasons including high fees and benefits that, in my opinion, are overstated by salespeople, variable annuities are an investment I often warn against." **If you suspect you might have a variable annuity, ask a fiduciary professional to examine your contract and make recommendations that are in your best interest.**

The Fixed Indexed Annuity: The Fixed Indexed Annuity (FIA) is the newest flavor to the annuity scene. It is sometimes called a hybrid annuity because it borrows positive elements from both the fixed and variable annuities mentioned above. First and foremost, this is a productive green money tool so you receive a contractual guarantee of principal and can never go backwards because the market goes backwards. But what about upside potential? This is where the word index comes into play. The FIA can credit interest based on market gains without the unpredictability of market loss.

What does Suze Orman have to say about the indexed annuity? On pages 511 and 513 respectively of "The Road to Wealth" she writes: "It was created to compete with very popular index funds, mutual funds that track a stock market index. I must admit I like the concept." Later, she adds: "If you do not want to take any risk but still want to play the stock market, a good, indexed annuity may be right for you."

The rest of this chapter is devoted to the features and benefits of this newer hybrid annuity so you can determine if an indexed option might be a good addition to your portfolio.

THE HYBRID APPROACH TO YOUR INCOME NEEDS

Today, you probably have savings in a variety of assets that you acquired over the years. But you may not have taken time to examine them and assess how they will support your retirement.

It's not about IF the market goes up or down, but WHEN it does. If it goes down at the wrong time for your 5- or 7-year retirement horizon, you could be in serious danger of not only losing principal but even more detrimental, completely outliving your money.

Each year, the market can only do one of three things:
1. Go up
2. Go down
3. Wind up flat

If you could remove any of those possible outcomes which one, would you remove? I bet you said #2, "go down" and in doing so you have just in most simplistic way described how a "no fee, safe growth" fixed indexed annuity works. There are only two outcomes for your account value it will be up or flat in any given year assuming you do not surrender the account or withdraw the 10% penalty free amount.

Ask yourself the following questions:
- How important is it for you to find a safe growth that's protected against market losses and has no fees associated with it to protect some of your savings?
- How important is it for you to have a steady stream of guaranteed cash flowing into your bank account every month?

If you are searching for the best way to fill your income gap, a fixed indexed annuity investment tool is likely a good option for you to consider. In fact, these annuities have many similar qualities to Social Security that give them the same look and feel as that reliable check you get every month. Most importantly, a fixed indexed annuity can be an efficient and profitable way to solve your income gap.

Let's say you have saved $100,000 and need it to generate income to meet your needs beyond your Social Security and pension check (if you're lucky enough to have one). You give $100,000 to a big, strong, safe insurance company, who in turn invests it to generate growth. When you use that $100,000 to buy a fixed indexed annuity, you are linking your money to an index. It could be the S&P 500, the Dow Jones Industrial Average or any number of indexes.

The following story illustrates how using an indexed annuity can fill your income gap and save you money:

> » *Georgie is 60 years old and is wondering how he can use his assets to provide him with retirement income. He has a $5,000 per month income need. If he starts withdrawing his Social Security benefit in six years at age 66, it will provide him with $2,200 per month. He also has a pension that kicks in at age 66 that will give him another $1,320 per month.*
>
> *That leaves an income gap of $2,800 without factoring inflation into the equation. If Georgie uses typical Green Money tools (cds, money markets etc.) to solve his income need, he will need to deposit $840,000 at 4% to generate that $2,800 per month. If he uses Red Money and withdraws monthly from an S&P 500 fund, he will run out of money in 10 years if the market performs like it did from 2000 to 2012. Suffering a market downturn like that during the period for which he is relying on it for retirement income will change his life, and not for the better.*
>
> *Working with a fiduciary retirement income specialist, to find a better way, Georgie discovered that he could take a hybrid approach to fill his income gap. His fiduciary professional recommended a fixed indexed annuity, another green money tool. This tool filled his income gap with only using $412,903, requiring him to spend $427,097 less money to accomplish his goal! Working with the right professional to find the most appropriate tools for him retirement needs saved Georgie over half a million dollars.*

DO YOU NEED AN INCOME RIDER?
Up to this point, the indexed annuity is a "no fee" investment. The insurance company makes their money on the "spread" just like the bank does with a CD. However, to generate income from the annuity, you select something called an income rider like Georgie did. If the goal is to create a guaranteed lifetime income stream for yourself or both you and your spouse, now or in the future, consider adding an income rider.

HOW DOES THE INCOME RIDER WORK?
Essentially, the insurance company creates a separate account from which they will base your income on while you have your money in their annuity. Your income rider value will be a larger number than your actual account value. And if you select the income rider now and do not need income until the future it will increase at a guaranteed rate (i.e. 7%) in value over time, providing you with a more guaranteed income when you're ready to turn on the income rider. The fixed index annuity with an income rider is simply a way you can create your own pension income. This will guarantee growth for guaranteed future income for the rest of your life and your spouses if married.

- **A recent innovation with Income Riders is the ability to double income if a chronic illness requires home health care or long-term care.** For example, if you are receiving $2,000 a month of guaranteed income from your annuity and you are unable to perform two out of six activities of daily living (ADL), the income would double to $4,000 a month for a period of time (i.e. 5 years) to help you meet some of those extra costs. After this time period, the income would revert to the original $2,000. This is a long-term care alternative, but not a replacement for traditional long-term care insurance.

It's crucial to choose companies that offer long-term care or home healthcare doubler that continues even if your account value reaches zero. Unfortunately, many companies offer "doublers", but most won't double your income once your account value reaches zero. Ensure you're with a company that guarantees your income will not only continue, but also will double regardless of the account balance ever reducing to zero.

ONE OF THE BEST THINGS ABOUT ANNUITIES: SURRENDER CHARGES

To encourage investors to leave their money in their annuities, insurance companies create surrender periods that protect their investments. If you remove more than the "penalty free" amount of money (typically 10 percent in year one declining over the term) from the annuity contract during the surrender period or "term" of the annuity, you will pay an early withdrawal or surrender penalty on the excess. A typical surrender period is between 5 and 10 years. If after three years you decide that you want your $100,000 back, the insurance company has that money tied up in bonds and other investments with the understanding that they would have it for another seven years if you elected the 10-year term that would provide higher upside potential than a shorter term. Because they will take a hit on removing the money from their investments prematurely, you will have to pay a surrender charge that makes up for their loss on any withdrawal more than the penalty free amount.

If your goal is "no fees" and "safe growth," a plain vanilla fixed index annuity is worth considering. It guarantees your principal won't decrease if the market declines, while offering higher upside potential by linking to an external index. However, be mindful of limited liquidity during the term due to surrender charges and penalties on withdrawals. After the surrender period, your money becomes fully liquid, and you can move 100% of it at any time. The insurance company aligns its investments with your surrender timeline.

However, **if your goal is guaranteed growth for future lifetime income**, the surrender charge is less of a concern because the annuity is meant for pension income, not early withdrawal. Taking a 10% withdrawal would reduce your guaranteed paychecks, defeating the purpose of the annuity. **If you leave your money in the annuity contract, you get a reliable monthly income no matter what happens in the market.** Once the surrender period has expired, you can move 100% of your money whenever you want. Your money becomes totally liquid again because the insurance company has used it in an investment that fit the timeline of your surrender period. For many people, this is an attractive tradeoff that can provide a creative solution for filling their income gap.

Annuities with income riders are investment tools that look and feel a bit like Social Security with an account value. Every year you wait to turn on your income, the income account value will continue to grow by a guaranteed specified rate. The larger your income account gets the bigger your paychecks will be.

When is an annuity with an income rider right for you? If you have an income gap and you're looking for a way to create guaranteed growth for guaranteed lifetime income without market risk, a good, fixed index annuity with an income rider could be the best solution for you. A good fiduciary retirement income planning specialist can help you make that determination by taking the time to listen closely to your situation and understand what your needs are as you enter retirement.

CREATING AN INCOME PLAN

Creating an income plan before retirement ensures lifetime income and maintains your lifestyle. An efficient plan will provide more security for future needs and help build your legacy. Here is a basic roadmap of what we have covered so far:

Review your income needs and look specifically at the shortfall you may have during each year of your retirement based on your Social Security income, and income from any other assets you have.

- Ask yourself where you are in the distribution phase. Is retirement one year away? 10 years away? The longer you let your pension annuity "cook" the bigger your paychecks will be.
- Determine how much money you need and how you need to structure your existing assets to provide for that need.
- If you have an asset that you need to generate income, consider options offered by purchasing a good Fixed Indexed annuity with an income rider.

CHAPTER 9 QUICK TIPS //

- Like ice cream, annuities come in different flavors. Use them as a piece of the portfolio pie, and make sure you have access to adequate amounts of liquidity.

- If you want a long-term care income doubler, ensure the annuity's income rider guarantees the doubling even if the account value hits zero.

10
TAXES IN RETIREMENT

"I am proud to be paying taxes in the United States. The only thing is—I could be just as proud for half the money."
— Arthur Godfrey

Taxes play a starring role in the theater of retirement planning. Everyone is familiar with taxes (you've been paying them your entire working life), but not everyone is familiar with how to make **tax planning** a part of their retirement strategy.

Taxes are taxes, right? You'll pay them before retirement, and you'll pay them during retirement. What's the difference? The truth is that a strategic approach to taxes can help you save money, protect your assets and ensure that your legacy remains intact.

The key is in planning. Tax planning and tax reporting are different; most people only report their taxes. Most CPAs and tax professionals simply fill out tax forms instead of conducting proactive tax planning throughout the year for their clients. Most people just complete their 1040s or use TurboTax and send them to the IRS. Using a CPA for tax reporting is essentially paying someone to record history. **One of the big problems with tax reporting is that it is not uncommon to harvest one extra dollar out of the wrong account at the wrong time and see it snowball in the $3.70 of income, subject to taxation.** Instead, be proactive with tax planning by analyzing your income sources to determine the optimal withdrawals from the proper buckets in order to minimize taxes during retirement. A fiduciary retirement income planner with the right software can help you make informed decisions and develop a forward-looking strategy. *Be sure to collaborate with a CPA or tax professional, before making any final decisions with strategic tax consulting provided by a fiduciary retirement income planner.*

TAXES AND RETIREMENT

When you retire, you shift from earning and accumulating assets to distributing them. This typically involves relying on Social Security, an employer sponsor retirement plan, IRAs, and some sort of pension for income. Most distributions from these sources are taxable, although exceptions exist, such as non-taxable Roth IRA distributions and partially taxable Social Security benefits.

For assets in an IRA or an employer sponsor plan (i.e. 401(k) or 403(b)) , you must begin taking required minimum distributions (RMDs) at a certain age due to the Secure Act 2.0. There is an exception for employer, sponsored plans. If you have reached RMD age, and you still have a 401(k) or 403(b) at your current employer you can delay RMD from that account until you officially retire.

Below are the current RMD rules under the Secure Act 2.0:
- If you were born between 1951 and 1959, you must start RMDs at age 73.

- If you were born in 1960 or later, you must start RMDs at age 75.

RMD amounts depend on your age and IRA balance. The government requires these withdrawals to generate tax, revenue.

If your IRA balance is large, RMDs could increase your taxable income and potentially place you in a higher tax bracket. This is where tax planning becomes advantageous. During the distribution phase, your income is predictable, consisting of RMDs, Social Security benefits, and other income-generating assets. ***The key is how much money you keep after taxes.*** If you reduce your taxes by 30%, 20%, or even 10%, you effectively earn that much more money by not paying it in taxes.

How do you save money on taxes? By having a plan. Your fiduciary retirement income planner can collaborate with your CPA to create a distribution plan that minimizes taxes and maximizes your annual net income.

BUILDING A TAX DIVERSIFIED PORTFOLIO

So far, so good: avoid taxes, maximize your net annual income and have a plan for doing it. When people decide to leverage the experience and resources of a financial professional, they may not be thinking of how distribution planning and tax planning will benefit their portfolios. Often more exciting prospects such as income annuities, investing in the market and structuring investments for growth rule the day. Taxes, however, play a crucial role in retirement planning. Achieving those tax goals requires knowledge of options, foresight and professional guidance.

Finding the path to a good tax plan isn't always a simple task. Every tax return you file is different from the one before it be- cause things constantly change. Your expenses are changing. Planned or unplanned purchases occur. Health care costs, medical bills, an inheritance, property purchases, reaching an age where RMDs kick in or travel—any number of things can affect how much income you report and how many deductions you take each year.

Preparing for the ever-changing landscape of your financial life requires a tax-diversified portfolio that can be leveraged to balance the incomes, expenditures and deductions that affect you each year. A financial professional will work with you to answer questions like these:

- Do you have a diversity of taxable, non-taxable and capital gains income planned for your retirement?
- Do you have a systematic plan to convert taxable accounts like traditional IRAs and 401(k)s into tax-free accounts like Roth IRAs?
- Is your portfolio strong enough and tax-diversified enough to adapt to an ever-changing (and usually increasing) tax code?

No one can be expected to know the entire U.S. tax code. But someone who is working with a team including CPAs and a Retirement Income Planning professional has an advantage over the average taxpayer who must start from square one on their own every year. Have you been taking advantage of all the deductions that are available to you?

PROACTIVE TAX PLANNING

The implications of proactive tax planning are far reaching and are larger than many people realize. Remember, doing your taxes in January, February, March or April means you are writing a history book. Planning your taxes in October, November or December means that you are writing the story as it happens. You can look at all the factors that are at play and make decisions that will impact your tax return *before* you file it.

Realizing that tax planning is an aspect of financial planning is an important leap to make. When you incorporate tax planning into your financial planning strategy, it becomes part of the way you maximize your financial potential. Paying less in taxes means you keep more of your money. Simply put, the more money you keep, the more of it you can leverage as an asset. This kind of planning can affect you at any stage of your life. If you are still working, are you contributing enough to maximize your company match? Are you contributing to a Roth IRA? Do you have life insurance and a plan to help leverage your assets to help cover home healthcare or long-term care in the future? Taxes and tax planning affect all investment tools. Partnering with a retirement income planner who collaborates with a CPA can help you build a comprehensive financial plan that integrates your investments and optimizes your assets for tax efficiency. Some years you might benefit from higher distributions due to your tax bracket, while in other years, taking less could be advantageous. Adapting your distributions to align with available deductions is key to smart tax planning. Professional guidance can enhance your income distribution strategy, allowing you to maximize tax efficiency. Remember, saving money on taxes is often more beneficial than earning more.

> » *When Gerald's father passed away, he discovered that he was the beneficiary of his father's $500,000 IRA. Gerald has a wife and four children, and he knew that his father had intended for a large portion of the IRA to go toward funding their college education.*
>
> *After Gerald's father's estate was distributed, Gerald, who is 50 years old and whose two oldest sons are entering college, liquidates the IRA. By doing so, his taxable income for that year puts him in a 37 percent tax bracket, immediately reducing the value of the asset to $315,000.*
>
> *Gerald's state taxes are an additional 5.75% percent. By the time the "tax man" is through, Gerald's income from*

the IRA will be taxed at 42.75% percent, leaving him with $213,750 of the original $500,000. While it would help contribute to the education of his children, it wouldn't come anywhere near completely paying for it, something the $500,000 could have easily done.

As the above example makes clear, leaving an asset to your beneficiaries can be more complicated than it may seem.

Here's an example of how taxes can significantly impact asset management:

> » John and Jordan, a 62-year-old couple, started working with a fiduciary retirement income planner in October. After structuring their assets to match their risk tolerance and create retirement income, they felt confident about their financial situation. They made decisions to maximize Social Security benefits, fill their income gap, and develop a customized investment strategy, including loss mitigation with their Fiduciary Retirement Income Planner.
>
> However, when asked about their tax planning, they realized they only relied on their CPA for annual tax filing versus doing any kind of tax planning. Their financial professional had a CPA strategic partner run a tax projection, which resulted in a tax plan saving them over $3,000. The CPA advised them to pay estimated taxes before the year's end to itemize it as a deduction, demonstrating the value of proactive tax planning.

This solution may not apply every year or to everyone, but it highlights how working with professionals and utilizing available resources can lead to a tax plan that saves money.

TAXES IN RETIREMENT

CHAPTER 10 QUICK TIPS //

- Know when you must start taking required minimum distributions (RMDs) from your retirement accounts and ensure you withdraw the correct amount annually to avoid penalties.

- Avoid the trap of deferring all withdrawals from qualified accounts until your RMD start date. While tax deferral seems beneficial, larger accounts can lead to higher taxes later. Consider a Roth Conversion plan.

- Don't neglect to build a tax diversified portfolio, including taxable, tax-deferred, and as many tax-free buckets as possible

11
TAX ALLOCATION

"Would you rather pay taxes on the seed or on the harvest? The seed is small, but the harvest is much bigger." – Ed Slott, CPA

Although the phrase "nothing is certain except for death and taxes" is most famously attributed to Benjamin Franklin, variations of this saying existed even before the country's first taxes were levied, and these words continue to ring true to this day. However, due to recent upheavals in the American financial landscape, this saying might need to be modified to, "nothing is certain except for death and *increasing* taxes."

DEBT AND EARNINGS
Currently, the national debt is increasing at an unprecedented rate, rising to levels never seen before and threatening serious harm to

the economy. In 2020, the national debt was $26.9 trillion*, and by August 2024 it had climbed to $35.1 trillion** which means the debt per taxpayer is over $268,000! It is projected by the end of 2024 our debt to national gross domestic product (GDP), which is basically the total value of all final good services produced within the United States will be 102%!*** Many economists believe that a sustainable economy exists at a maximum debt to GDP of approximately 80%.

The significance of these two numbers lies within the contrast. The national debt is the amount that needs to be repaid; this can be thought of as the government's credit card balance. In other words, the GDP represents the gross taxable income available to the government. If debts are increasing at a rate greater than the gross income available for taxation, then the only way to make up the difference is to increase the rate at which the gross income is being taxed.

WHAT DOES THE SOLUTION LOOK LIKE?

Unfortunately, the general public faces a no-win situation. Printing money fuels inflation, devaluing the U.S. dollar and reducing wealth, while cutting entitlements strips millions of expected benefits. The remaining option, well-known to the government, is raising taxes.

How do you prepare? Why spend so much time reassuring you that taxes will likely increase? Because you have an opportunity to take action. Now is the time to prepare for future changes by implementing tax-advantaged retirement planning. We know current tax rates, and if the 2017 Trump tax cuts aren't extended,

---

* *investopedia.com/us-national-debt-by-year-7499291*

** *usdebtclock.org*

*** *https://www.whitehouse.gov/wp-content/uploads/2023/03/ap_20_borrowing_-fy2024.pdf*

rates and brackets will rise in January 2026, with the standard deduction basically being cut in half. Taxes are essentially "on sale" now, strengthening the case for Roth conversions before 2026, though the future remains uncertain.

The truth of the matter is that you make more money by saving on taxes than you do by making more money. The simplistic logic of this statement makes sense when you discover it takes a $1.50 in earnings to put that same dollar, saved in taxes, back in your pocket.* This simple concept becomes extremely valuable to people in retirement and those living on fixed incomes.

THE BENEFITS OF DIVERSIFICATION

Heading into retirement, you should be situated within a diversified tax landscape. The point to spending your whole life accumulating wealth is not to see how big the number is on paper, but rather to be an exercise in how much you put in your pocket after removing it from the paper.

To truly understand tax diversification, you must understand what types of money exist and how each of these will be treated during accumulation and, most importantly, during distribution. The following is a brief summary:

1. Free money
2. Tax-advantaged money
3. Tax-deferred money
4. Taxable money
    a. Ordinary income
    b. Capital gains and qualified dividends

FREE MONEY

Free money is always beneficial, regardless of tax treatment, because it increases your overall wealth. Many employers enhance

---

Assuming a 33 percent effective tax rate

retirement savings by offering matching contributions. For example, if you earn $50,000 and contribute 3% ($1,500), and your employer matches it with another $1,500, it's free money, so take all that you can get!

TAX-ADVANTAGED MONEY

Tax-advantaged money is the next best thing to free money because you reduce current taxes. While you must earn it, it's taxed less than regular income. Some municipal bonds, a common form of tax advantage, money, offer federal, state, or both tax advantages. However, states may tax interest on out-of-state bonds, impacting their benefits and liquidity. Municipal bond interest also counts toward your modified adjusted gross income (MAGI) for Social Security, potentially taxing your benefits, and it's considered in the alternative minimum tax (AMT) applicable.

TAX-FREE MONEY: ROTH IRA

Roth accounts, established by the 1997 Taxpayer Relief Act and named after Senator William Roth, are one of the best tax assets, along with life insurance, yet both are often underutilized. They offer tax-advantaged growth and income, with the main difference from traditional IRAs being when taxes are actually paid.

In a traditional plan, contributions are made pre-tax, meaning you don't pay taxes on the earnings now, but you do when you withdraw in retirement, which can increase your taxable income and affect Social Security taxes, the Alternative Minimum Tax (AMT), and Medicare premiums. Roth accounts and cash value life insurance, however, are funded with after-tax dollars, so withdrawals in retirement are tax-free and don't affect these calculations.

A useful analogy is that of a farmer: Would you prefer to pay taxes on $5,000 worth of seeds now or $50,000 worth of harvested crops later? The Roth account is like paying taxes on the seeds, with no tax due at harvest time.

So why doesn't everyone have a Roth? This is likely due to contribution limits; for example, in 2024, individuals with a Modified Adjusted Gross Income (MAGI) over $146,000 (single) or $230,000 (joint) can't contribute unless they use a little known technique, called "the back- door, Roth". The "back door- Roth" is simply a strategy where a high-income earner who would not normally qualify to contribute to a Roth IRA establishes a nondeductible, traditional IRA and then converts it to a Roth. Discuss this type of transaction with your CPA or tax professional before completing it.

There's really no reason why everyone should not be building as many tax-free buckets of money as possible utilizing the Roth IRA. There are four ways people can get more money into Roth buckets:

1. **Contributions:** if your earnings are below the income limits discussed above.

2. **Back door Roth:** if you're a high-income earner exceeding the contribution limits

3. **Roth conversions:** There is no limit on the amount individuals, working or retired, can convert to Roth IRAs.

4. **401(k) Roth**: Most employers have this option available and there are no income limits for a Roth 401(k) contributions.

One caveat with Roth 401(k)s is that they don't start the five-year clock for tax-free distributions on gains, which only begins after the later of five years or age 59 ½. To ensure that the clock starts, establish an individual Roth account ASAP assuming you don't already have one.

TAX-DEFERRED MONEY

Most people are familiar with tax-deferred money, such as traditional IRAs, employer-sponsored retirement plans, and non-qualified annuities. In these accounts, earnings grow tax-free until you withdraw them. When distributed, the money is taxed as ordinary income, potentially leading to additional tax liabilities and expenses (i.e. higher rates, additional Social Security tax, pre-age 59.5 penalties).

TAXABLE MONEY

Taxable money includes all other income that is taxed both now and when received. Of these four types of money, it really comes down to two distinct classifications: taxable and tax advantaged. The key difference is how much money you keep after taxes.

In the end, most people spend their lives accumulating wealth through the best known, if not the only vehicle they know which is a tax-deferred account. This account is most likely a 401(k) or 403(b) plan offered through your employer and may be supplemented with an IRA that was established at one point or another. As the years go by, people blindly throw money into these accounts in an effort to save for a retirement that they someday hope to reach.

The truth is most people have an age selected for when they would like to retire but spend their lives wondering if they will ever be able to quit working. To answer this question, you must understand how much money you will have available to contribute to your needs. **In other words, you need to know what your after-tax income will be during this period.**

All else being equal, it would not matter if you put your money into a taxable, tax-deferred, or tax-advantaged account as long as income tax rates never change, and outside factors are never an event. The net amount you receive in the end would be the same. Unfortunately, this will never be the case. It's likely taxes will increase in the future, potentially equating to higher rates in retirement than during peak earning years. **The way to insulate yourself against future legislative risk of higher taxes down the road is through converting and creating as many tax-free buckets of money as possible.**

CHAPTER 11 QUICK TIPS //

- The future of U.S. taxation is uncertain. You know what the tax rate and landscape is today, but you don't know what's in store for tomorrow so don't fall victim to just "tax reporting."

- Most people know about tax-deferred retirement savings like traditional IRAs. Acting now can prepare you for higher taxes by restructuring your assets to include free and tax-advantaged money.

- Consider starting a strategic Roth conversion plan for your traditional IRAs, 401(k)s, and 403(b)s to build more tax-free wealth for you and your loved ones.

12
TAX AVOIDANCE VS. TAX EVASION

There's a big difference between tax avoidance and tax evasion. Can you guess the difference? That's right—jail! And you might not like your roommate either.

Louis Brandeis provides one of the best examples illustrating how tax avoidance works. Brandeis was Associate Justice on the Supreme Court of the United States from 1916 to 1939. Born in Louisville, Kentucky, Brandeis was an intelligent man with a touch of country charm. He described tax planning this way:

"I live in Alexandria, Virginia. Near the Court Chambers, there is a toll bridge across the Potomac. When in a rush, I pay the dollar toll and get home early. However, I usually drive outside the downtown section of the city and cross the Potomac on a free bridge.

The bridge was placed outside the downtown Washington, D.C. area to serve a useful social service—getting drivers to drive the extra mile and help alleviate congestion during the rush hour.

If I went over the toll bridge and through the barrier without paying a toll, I would be committing tax evasion.

If I drive the extra mile and drive outside the city of Washington to the free bridge, I am using a legitimate, logical and suitable method of tax avoidance, and I am performing a useful social service by doing so.

*The tragedy is that **few people know that the free bridge exists**."*

Brandeis' story illustrates the importance of proactive tax planning. Just as he chose the free bridge, you have the option to incorporate tax planning into your financial strategy to avoid unnecessary taxes. This might involve converting traditional IRAs to Roth IRAs, using charitable donations, or leveraging itemized deductions to offset taxes.

ROTH IRA CONVERSIONS

The attractive qualities of Roth IRAs may have prompted you to explore the possibility of converting some of your qualified IRAs and 401(k)s into a Roth account. Another important difference between the accounts is how they treat Required Minimum Distributions (RMDs). As discussed earlier, if you were born between 1951 and 1959, you must start RMDs from your qualified retirement accounts at age 73. If you were born in 1960 or later, RMDs begin at age 75. Unless you use a qualified charitable distribution (QCD) strategy, your RMDs are taxable. Roth IRAs have no RMDs for the original owner, but non-spouse beneficiaries must take RMDs, which remain tax-free.

While having a Roth IRA is advantageous, converting assets from a traditional IRA to a Roth IRA can be challenging. A traditional IRA grows tax-deferred until withdrawal, while Roth

IRA contributions are taxed upfront, not on withdrawal. When transferring assets from a traditional IRA to a Roth IRA, taxes apply to the conversion amount.

Many people consider Roth conversions because traditional IRAs can have significant tax implications due to high RMDs. For instance, with a $500,000 IRA, the RMD at age 73 is about $19,000, which is mandatory and could affect your tax bracket and Social Security taxation. By converting to a Roth IRA, you pay taxes now and benefit from tax-free growth later. This strategy is often likened to paying taxes on seeds instead of the harvest: you pay taxes on the smaller amount now and avoid taxes on the larger sum later. With a Roth IRA, you pay taxes once, and you and your heirs also benefit from tax-free distributions.

It's a powerful tool. Here's a simple example to show you how powerful it can be:

> *Imagine you convert a traditional IRA to a Roth IRA, paying a 25% tax on the conversion. If the Roth IRA doubles in value over the next 10 years, your effective tax rate on the original amount is just 12.5%. Plus, you won't have to worry about RMDs increasing your taxes on Social Security, higher tax rates on future RMDs, or taxes on distributions for you and your beneficiaries…pretty sweet, huh?*

The prospect of tax-advantaged income is appealing no doubt. While you have to pay a conversion tax to transfer your assets, you also have turned taxable income into tax-free retirement money that you can let grow as long as you want without being required to withdraw it.

There are options, however, that address this problem. Much like the Brandeis story, there may be a "free bridge" option for many investors.

Here are some things to consider before converting to a Roth IRA:

- Converting before retirement may result in higher taxes due to peak earning years. However, if you itemize your deductions, have dependents, a mortgage (hopefully both will be gone in retirement), and charitable deductions, those can help to offset some the taxes on Roth conversions.

- Waiting to convert after you or your spouse (if married) has retired may be a time when you have less taxable income, allowing for larger Roth conversions.

- When converting into retirement, be mindful of the amount you are converting after age 63, as it could impact your Medicare premiums. You may be "okay" with that trade-off, but it's important to consider and not be caught off guard by a Medicare premium increase.

There are a couple strategies when it comes to handling the taxes due for Roth conversions. The first is if you have the ability to pay the cost of the tax conversion with outside money, it will give you the most long-term bang for your buck because 100% of the amount you convert goes into Roth. However, many people choose another strategy that may be more palatable, and that is simply taking the funds for the Roth conversion and letting the IRA pay the tax.

For example, if you're in a net effective 20% tax bracket, simply convert $100,000, withhold $20,000 for taxes and you end up with $80,000 in your Roth IRA and did not have to come out of pocket money, you simply let the traditional IRA pay the tax. Your fiduciary retirement income planner, with the help of a CPA, may be able to provide you with options like after-tax money, itemized deductions or other situations that can pose effective tax avoidance options.

Here are a few strategies that can help offset the taxes due to Roth conversions:

- **Medical Expenses:** *If your medical expenses exceed 7.5% of your Adjusted Gross Income (AGI), you can use them to offset the tax from a Roth conversion.*

- **Net Operating Losses** *(NOLs): Small business owners with NOLs can carry them forward to offset the taxable income from Roth conversions.*

- **Charitable Giving:** *By increasing your charitable donations in the year of a Roth conversion, you can reduce your taxable income and effectively avoid taxation on the conversion.*

Not all scenarios will work for everyone, but there are many ways to offset conversion taxes. Your financial and tax professionals can help you understand these options. If you have a traditional IRA, consider Roth conversions as you approach retirement to maximize your savings and keep more of your retirement money in your pocket instead of the government's.

ADDITIONAL TAX BENEFITS OF ROTH IRAS

Not only do Roth IRAs provide you with tax-advantaged growth, but they also give you a tax diversified landscape that allows you to maximize your distributions. Chances are that no matter the circumstances, you will have taxable income and other assets subject to taxation. *But if you have a Roth IRA, you have the unique ability to manage your Adjusted Gross Income (AGI), because you have a tax-advantaged income option!*

TO CONVERT OR NOT TO CONVERT?

Conversions aren't just for retirees; you can convert at any time. Whether to stick with a traditional IRA, convert to a Roth, or have a combination depends on your individual circumstances, including your income, tax bracket, and deductions.

The bottom line is that having a tax diversified landscape gives you options. Do yourself a favor and *plan* your taxes instead of *reporting* them!

CHAPTER 12 QUICK TIPS //

- There are many ways to reduce your taxes. Being smart about your Roth IRA conversion is one of the main ways to do so.

- Large Roth conversions sweet spot for retirees is age 62 or earlier, to avoid potential "spikes" in your Medicare premiums.

- Work with a fiduciary retirement specialist to determine your annual Roth conversion amount and always consult your CPA or tax professional before proceeding.

13
YOU'RE RETIRED...NOW WHAT?

"Most folks are about as happy as they make up their minds to be."
– Abraham Lincoln

Retirement is the pinnacle of a successful career, but there is a long road to get there. It takes hard work, commitment, and strategy. Retirement is your chance to accomplish goals and create new meaning for your life. Not everyone enters retirement with a clear vision, however. Imagine climbing up a mountain and focusing on reaching the top. The goal of getting to the summit is your motivation. You might be so focused on reaching the top that you forget to think about other things like the hike back down. Now, imagine that climb is your journey to retirement. I have seen so many people come into our office so focused on reaching retirement that they forget to think about what they will do during the days, months, and years that follow. Retirement significantly changes your daily life, and it takes proactive planning to be prepared.

A PLAN FOR YOUR MOST VALUABLE ASSET
In addition to investments and income planning, you will want to **create a strategy for your time.** Many people do not expect to miss work when they retire but find themselves feeling lost within a few months of retirement. Work gives people structure and a purpose. Think about runners who train for a marathon. They spend months training and then run the marathon in a day. However, once they have completed the marathon, they keep running. Why? Because they are used to running. They have developed a good habit and exercise feels good.

Work is similar because it gives people a way to use their skills and feel good about themselves. To avoid becoming bored, you are going to want to continue using your skills once you are retired. Luckily, there are a lot of ways outside of working a full-time job to feel fulfilled.

Millions of American spend the bulk of their lives working, planning, and setting goals. Their lives are full of projects, deadlines, and challenges that keep them occupied and growing. Many people lose their sense of purpose when they retire because they have not had time to think about their purpose outside of work or what they want to do next. People with successful careers often struggle to transition to retirement because they are used to living a fast-paced life. You will want to create a plan for **YOUR MOST VALUABLE ASSET** (not your money but rather your time) during retirement or else you will end up bored and discouraged very soon after retiring.

Retirement is an opportunity to find a new purpose or build on an existing one. Before retirement, most workers are living a life of "personal" time poverty. When you are working, you have eight hours for sleep, eight hours for work, and eight hours for time off during the week. You have Saturday for leisure, family, fun, and projects. Then Sunday is left for a day of worship, rest, additional chores, projects, and sports. After retirement, every day is a Saturday; there is an additional 8 to 10 hours each day, depending on individual work and commute schedules, that must be filled with something else. You are gaining an additional 40 to 50 hours each week that are now available to do whatever you want. Realistically, there is only so much grass you can cut and only so much pickleball or golf that you can play. If you spend the bulk of your time sleeping, lounging, eating, and binge-watching TV, you will be left overweight, overspending, and wishing you never retired.

Retirement is a season of your life that you have worked hard towards and dreamed of for many years. Stepping into it without a plan for your time is a recipe for boredom and depression within about 60 days after you retire. I do not want to see that happen to you. People are designed to grow and to be active. **The law of life is to grow or die.** You will want to continue growing during your retirement whether it is spiritually, mentally, physically, or all three. You do not want to be a sitting ship docked at the harbor during retirement. You want to be in the ocean sailing free. Simply put, it is your responsibility to make the most of your retirement.

You are made for growth and useful purpose; do not let your career be your last meaningful chapter when you still have so much left to give. *Just as you had a financial game plan for retirement that was thoughtful and required discipline to retire, you must also have a plan for your time so you can make the most out of it in retirement.*

This book is a call to action to start planning your retirement early and a guide for how to start thinking through your retirement goals. **What do you want to accomplish during your retirement?** People are living longer and having longer retirements as a result. You have been preparing financially for retirement, but now it is time to start preparing emotionally. You should start thinking about how you are going to spend your time when you are retired well before retirement. I am confident retirement can be one of the best chapters of your life if you are prepared.

CREATING THE VISION

"Where there is no vision, the people perish…" – Proverbs 29:18 KJV

A fulfilling retirement requires a vision. You do not want to be wandering aimlessly throughout the last chapter of your life when you still have so much to offer. To keep your life fresh and fulfilled, you must have a plan to fill your time. This is your opportunity to pursue personal passions, fun hobbies, new experiences, deepening relationships, and building new ones. These are all great ways to keep your mind sharp, your body strong and healthy, and to give your life real meaning and purpose.

You may be surprised by the number of people who come through our office and give us the deer in the headlight stare, when we ask them these questions: **"What is your retirement vision? How do you plan to spend your time in retirement? What does your ideal retirement look like?"** They have not given it very much thought at all. You may even know someone who has retired only to re-enter the workforce after a relatively short stint in retirement because they are bored. They entered the so called "Golden Years" and, because they did not have a plan for how they would spend their time, they decided to go back to work. They were not prepared to replace the structure, meaning, purpose, and sense of accomplishment that work provided. Now do not get me wrong, there are many people who have part-time work that is low stress and performed on their terms as part of their retirement plan, and that is great as long as that job is part of your plan. However, going to work because you cannot find enough fulfillment in what should be the very best season of life called retirement is simply sad, and very much avoidable with a well-thought-out plan.

You have so much to contribute, and there's only so much leisure time a person can enjoy. Think about what is important to you. Do you have fun hobbies? What are you passionate about? What does your ideal retirement look like to you? Have you always dreamed about going on a mission trip? Your work has provided you with structure and self-worth. Now, you will need to develop a new purpose. You are going to be okay, but this is a huge adjustment. You will want to be prepared for this transition. Retirement is about so much more than sleeping in and avoiding traffic. You have been living in time poverty, and now you have an abundance of time to make a difference that matters to you.

THE POWER OF POSITIVE THINKING

The first thing to realize about a happy retirement is that happiness typically results from good circumstances that come and go all throughout life. Happiness is temporary, but as the quote at the beginning of this chapter states **"people are about as happy as they make up their minds to be."** You can live with joy which comes from the inside regardless of the circumstances life throws at you. I cannot say it better than the Bible:

"Be ye transformed by the renewing of your mind"
— *Romans 12:2 KJV*

The Bible also says laughter is good medicine so go out and laugh more. Start transforming your thoughts from negative to positive. Just like any habit, it may take some time to recognize a negative thought, capture it, and reframe it. However, the more you practice, the more natural it will become. When you notice a negative thought, say, "No, I'm not going to think that way," and replace it with positive thought, especially before you process that thought and into word or action.

Be sensitive to what you let into your mind. Read good books, watch good shows, and hang out with positive people. I recommend everyone read a great little book called *As A Man Thinketh* by James Allen. The book says, "thoughts attract that upon which they are directed," so start healthy habits today. Feed your mind with mental vitamins, exercise your body, and keep moving. Two other classics, I highly recommend are The Bible and The Power of Positive Thinking by Norman, Vincent Peale.

Make a commitment to service and making a positive difference in the lives of others part of your weekly, if not daily, routine, and you will see the fruit of a few simple healthy habits change the world around you from negative to positive. If you're looking for ideas locally here in Jackson County I can recommend two phenomenal organizations. The first is **iServe Ministries**, a local nonprofit with two missions. The first is to end generational poverty in Jackson County, Georgia. They are always looking for volunteers to help with their monthly food trucks and to pack "backpacks of love" full of food for kids to take home from school. Their second mission is to end homelessness in Jackson County through their "Village of Hope" initiative. You can learn more about their programs by visiting iserveministries.org

The second organization is **Legacy Youth Mentoring**, part of the Jackson County school system. Hundreds of local children are seeking men and women to invest in their lives as mentors. Jeff Grant, one of the founders of iServe Ministries, encouraged me for years to mentor a young man, but I always made excuses, telling myself, "I don't have the time." One day, I reflected on how good God has been to me by placing spiritual fathers in my life to guide me at critical times, and I wanted to pay that forward. For the past 3 1/2 years, I've been mentoring a young man named Sebastian, and it has been one of the most fulfilling experiences of my life. If you have interest, I would encourage you to reach out to Lisa Stephens, who is the mentoring coordinator at lisa@legacyyouthmentoring.org.

You have the power to transition from worry to being free of fear, and you can live happily and worry-free. The choice is yours to make.

THE JOY OF MEANINGFUL RELATIONSHIPS

Relationships are an important source of joy during retirement. It has been said that *"the quality of our lives is determined by the quality of our relationships."* We, as humans, are made for relationships: first with our creator God Almighty, and second with other people. During retirement, you are rich with time. You are no longer fighting ever worsening traffic in a painful commute or juggling the pressure of a stressful job. In retirement, you have the freedom to invest in existing relationships and build new ones as well. You also have an opportunity to focus on spiritual growth if you have neglected the spiritual side of life because of a busy career.

You are now able to give your family and friends the best of you. While you were working, they may have been receiving the "left- overs" of your "life force": both time and energy. In retirement, you now have freedom and flexibility to help more and be more involved. For example, you could start scheduling more meals with family and friends. You could also consider visiting those without family in senior centers or nursing homes, mentoring through youth organizations, or possibly serving your community by volunteering at a food bank. Retirement is an opportunity to make a positive difference in the lives of others. I can promise you, if you invest some of your time in the lives of others, you will discover or rediscover the incredible joy that can only be found through meaningful relationships. This is what is called purpose and fulfillment through investing your time in the lives of others.

THE PURSUIT OF EXCELLENT HEALTH

I have yet to see a U-Haul being pulled by a hearse or luggage racks on a casket. When we permanently exit this "earth suit" we call a body, you cannot take any of your wealth and possessions with you. I do not care how much wealth you have accumulated; if you do not have your health, what good is it? Your heirs will appreciate all your years of toil and stress, but I doubt your plan was to amass wealth over your working career and then shortly thereafter pass.

It's a little like what I used to tell our children when they were younger about brushing their teeth: "Just brush and floss the ones you want to keep." You see brushing and flossing are good health habits. *When it comes to getting in shape and staying in shape, you must make physical exercise and healthy choices a habit.* For example, maybe you have never walked your driveway, the neighborhood or around a local park, and you make the decision to go for a walk. You cannot just do it once to stay healthy. It is the same as brushing your teeth or taking a bath; you really should do it once a week, right? No! You get the point. You have one body to live in while you are here on this earth. Make a plan and start today by getting your body moving and filling it with fuel worthy of someone you love. Your health is going to greatly determine what your retirement looks like.

BECOMING AND REMAINING DEBT FREE

Being debt free is an important component of being financially fit. My first book covered a lot about the new financial rules of retirement. Just like the end of movie, life goes on after the happy ending; once you retire, you have an exciting new story to live. The goal is not just to retire but to stay financially fit throughout retirement. I love seeing our clients go into retirement 100% debt free; they are the happiest and most financially secure ones because debt is simply bondage. Having debt inputs people at a greater risk of not having enough money coming in monthly to truly do everything they have always hoped to do in retirement.

Make a plan to be as debt free as possible before you step over that line into retirement or shortly after retirement. Set a goal for where you want to be and put a plan into action to pay off all consumer debt and even your primary residence. After my wife and I made the decision and put a plan into action, it took us just three years to write the final mortgage check and become debt-free at age 51. A friend of mine conquer the same feat at age 33 which is truly remarkable. I see it all the time in our firm. Someone's debt load prevents them from retiring when they would truly like too. Start tackling your debt today; do not wait to create a plan to pay off high-interest rate consumer debt. Only when you have debt eliminated will you know the joy of being completely financially free.

Once you are debt free, it is important to stay debt free throughout retirement. It is critical that you stay focused on not overspending, ultimately running a greater risk of outliving your money. When you set up your income plan, make sure the bulk of your core income is coming in from what we call "Sure Things": employer pensions, Social Security, and good pension annuities. Use your market-based investments to help create a rising stream of income in the future to offset inflation and to increase your long-term financial security. Think about it: if the bulk of your core lifestyle income is coming from "Sure Things" versus "Maybes" and we go through another 2008, great recession, or depression, you will still be able to sleep happy and worry free at night. Create a spending plan with recreation and travel built into it and live within your means. If you have a good year in the stock market, consider carving off some profit and doing a little extra that year.

CHAPTER 13 QUICK TIPS //

- You can never truly be financially free until you are debt-free! Create and implement a wise plan today to eliminate as much debt as possible before you step into retirement.

- Invest your extra time in retirement by building and creating new meaningful relationships. Look for volunteer organizations where you can contribute and add value.

- Commit to RETIRE STRONGER; mentally, physically, relationally, spiritually, and financially, which are the most important aspects of your life!

14
YOUR LEGACY BEYOND DOLLARS AND CENTS

"All good men and women must take responsibility to create legacies that will take the next generation to a level we could only imagine."
— Jim Rohn

If you are like most people, estate planning is probably not a top priority. You're focused on retirement income, managing assets, and living life. However, if you don't plan your legacy, someone else will—usually the IRS, lawyers, executors, and courts. And they won't have your beneficiaries' best interests at heart.

A legacy is more than the sum of the financial assets you have accumulated. It is the lasting impression you make on those you leave behind. The dollar and cents are just a small part of a legacy you leave behind. It includes the values, stories, and shared experiences you impart. For example, an estate may pay for college, but a legacy teaches the importance of education, perseverance, spiritual growth, generosity, compassion, and being a productive member of society.

A legacy may also include family heirlooms or items of emotional significance, like a piece of art, family photos, or keepsakes. When planning your legacy, consider both financial benefits and the personal elements you wish to pass on to others.

A key reason to plan your legacy is to maintain family harmony when dealing with death, money, and inheritance. Lack of planning can lead to significant conflict within a family.

Many delay legacy planning until a major life event, like a grandchild's birth, a serious diagnosis, or a loved one's death. Waiting can add emotional stress and hinder clear decision-making. Creating a plan now while all is well ensuring your assets are transferred as you wish.

THE BENEFITS OF PLANNING YOUR LEGACY

Distributing your assets, whether property, stocks, IRAs, 401(k)s, or liquid assets, can be complicated without clear instructions. Without a plan, it will cost more and take longer. Planning your legacy ensures your assets are transferred with minimal delay and confusion. Draft a clear plan early to preserve your wishes and avoid leaving these decisions to family, attorneys, and the courts. Thinking about passing on is difficult; it is a hard subject to tackle. **It reminds us that life is short.** And the relatively complicated nature of sorting through your assets can feel like a daunting task. But one thing is for sure: it is impossible for your assets to be transferred or distributed the way you want at the end of your life if you don't have a plan. **You do not have to tackle all of this in one day;** in fact, I highly recommend doing it over a period of time, breaking it up so you do not get overwhelmed. **Making a Legacy Plan Starts with a Simple List.**

Here are some helpful steps to take first:

- Get a clear picture of your assets by understanding and organizing them
- Make sure you have the correct beneficiary designated for each one of your assets. Beneficiary provisions, supersede anything stated in a will or trust.
- Designate power of attorney for health and financial decisions

MAKING A PLAN

When your income needs are met and you have sufficient standby money for emergencies, travel, or extra expenses, whatever remains becomes your financial legacy.

If you haven't communicated and put in writing your legacy distribution desires, it will be to your loved one's detriment. Managing a legacy involves more than just reading a will and dividing an estate; it includes tax issues and other decisions. Educate yourself and work with fiduciary financial professionals, especially an estate planning attorney, to ensure efficient preservation and distribution.

Begin by asking yourself and an estate planning attorney: Do I have or need the following?

- **A Will:** If not, the state you die in has written one for you, and trust me, you will not like the outcome.
- **A Living Will:** (Advance Directive): Specifies your wishes regarding medical treatment if you become incapacitated and unable to communicate your decisions.
- **A Durable Power of Attorney:** Appoints someone to make financial decisions on your behalf if you become incapacitated.

- **A Healthcare Power of Attorney** (Medical Power of Attorney): Appoints someone to make medical decisions for you if you are unable to do so.

- **A HIPAA Authorization:** Allows designated individuals to access your medical records and information.

- **A Revocable Living Trust:** Helps manage your assets during your lifetime and specifies how they should be distributed after your death, often avoiding probate.

- **Current Beneficiary Designations:** Ensures retirement accounts, life insurance policies, and other assets with beneficiary designations are up-to-date and aligned with your goals.

- **A Letter of Intent:** Provides additional instructions or information regarding your wishes, such as funeral arrangements or personal messages to loved ones.

- **Guardianship Designations:** Specifies who should care for your minor children if both parents are deceased or incapacitated.

The answers to these questions are imperative if you want control over asset distribution, to preserve family harmony, and achieve your legacy goals.

LIFE INSURANCE: AN IMPORTANT LEGACY TOOL

One of the most powerful legacy tools you can leverage is a good life insurance policy. Life insurance is a highly efficient legacy tool because it creates money when it is needed the most.

There are many unique benefits of life insurance that can help you while living and help your beneficiaries get the most out of your legacy. Some of them include:

- Providing a tax-free bucket of money (the death benefit) that can be used for home healthcare or long-term care needs
- Providing beneficiaries with a tax-free, liquid asset.
- Covering the costs associated with your death.
- Providing income for your dependents.
- Covering expenses such as tuition or mortgage down payments for your children or grandchildren.

Few people want life insurance, but almost everyone values what it provides. Life insurance uniquely creates funds when they're needed most. While money can't ease the pain of losing a loved one, it offers options during difficult times—options that wouldn't exist without it.

> » *Melissa spent 20 years building a small business, with her three children, Eric, Ashlynn and Makenzie,—working part-time during high school. After college, only Makenzie returned to work full-time, eventually taking over when Melissa retired. While Melissa can retire comfortably on Social Security and shop income, the business represents nearly her entire financial legacy. She wants Makenzie to own the business but also wants to leave an equal legacy to all three children.*
>
> *Dividing the business evenly would disrupt its operations, so Melissa buys a life insurance policy. Eric and Ashlynn will receive their inheritance in cash via tax-free, death benefit, while Makenzie inherits the business intact. This allows Melissa to treat her children fairly and ensure Makenzie continues the family business.*

If you have a life insurance policy but you haven't looked at it in a while, you may not know how it operates, how much it is worth, and how it will be distributed to your beneficiaries. You may also need to update your beneficiaries on your policy. Here's an example of why:

> » When Lulu turned 88, her daughter finally convinced her to meet with a financial professional to help organize her assets and get her legacy in order. Although Lulu is reluctant to let a stranger in on her personal finances, she ends up very glad that she did.
>
> In the process of listing Lulu's assets and her beneficiaries, her professional finds a man's name listed as the beneficiary of an old life insurance annuity that she owns. It turns out, the man is Lulu's ex-husband who is still alive. Had Lulu passed away before her ex-husband, the annuities and any death benefits that came with them, would have been passed on to her ex-husband.

In short, without a comprehensive review of your policy, you don't really know where the money will go or to whom it will go.

If you don't have a life insurance policy but are looking for options to maintain and grow your legacy, speaking with a professional can show you the benefits of life insurance. Many people don't consider buying a life insurance policy until some event in their life triggers it, like the loss of a loved one, an accident or a health condition.

MAKE YOUR WISHES KNOWN

Your legacy includes more than property, money, and investments. It encompasses personal items, values, beliefs, family history, and wishes. **Beyond a will, it's crucial to communicate your wishes for your personal legacy.** This helps your family make decisions that honor you and give meaning to what you leave behind. A professional can help you organize this.

Think about your:
- Personal stories / recollections
- Values
- Personal items of emotional significance
- Financial assets

WORKING WITH A PROFESSIONAL

Maximizing life insurance benefits begins with choosing the right policy and provider. With so many options, a trusted financial professional can guide you in selecting a policy that meets your goals. If you already have one, they can review it, explain the premium, guarantees, and features, and help make any necessary adjustments.

As life changes, your legacy plan should adapt. New children, grandchildren, divorces, or remarriages may require updates. A professional will regularly review your legacy assets to ensure they reflect your current wishes.

CHAPTER 14 QUICK TIPS //

- Get your estate planning documents in order and create a will. If you don't, the state will create one for you, and you won't like the outcome. Remember it's all about family harmony when you're no longer here.

- Consult an estate planning attorney. Your Retirement Income Specialist can likely arrange a complimentary consultation to get started.

- Your legacy encompasses more than just the physical assets left behind for your children. It also includes the ideals and values important to you.

- Life insurance offers tax-free, liquid assets for long-term or home healthcare needs and can greatly enhance your legacy for your beneficiaries.

15
CHOOSING A FINANCIAL PROFESSIONAL

As you begin your retirement journey, having a team of trusted fiduciaries is essential. It's important to know what you're looking for early on. While many can manage your money, not everyone is qualified to craft a comprehensive holistic retirement plan.

Seek a team that prioritizes your interests, is dedicated to your goals, and asks a lot of great questions. The specific tools they use matter less than their commitment to crafting the right plan that results in your success. A team of good professionals should consider your entire financial picture, helping you manage risk, secure retirement income, and support ongoing wealth accumulation.

Financial tools may change, but the principles of wise retirement planning are timeless. Choosing the right team is imperative because they manage the assets that fuel your retirement lifestyle and shape your legacy. So, how do you find the right one?

HOW TO FIND RETIREMENT INCOME PLANNING PROFESSIONALS YOU CAN TRUST

Working with professional Retirement Income Specialists is not the same as simply calling a broker to trade stocks. This level of planning requires your active involvement in finding a team you can truly trust with your financial future. While the process may take effort, it's worth it. Though no one can choose for you, the following information can help guide your decision.

NARROWING THE FIELD

Choose the type of professionals you want to work with.

Be cautious of anyone calling themselves a "planner" or "advisor," which can be misleading since an insurance agent or a stockbroker who just passed their exam yesterday without formal education or experience can call themselves either.

Ensure credibility by choosing professionals with credentials like CPA (Certified Public Accountant), CFP® (CERTIFIED FINANCIAL PLANNER™), RIA (Registered Investment Advisors) or IAR (Investment Advisory Affiliate). Credentialed professionals must meet both education and experience requirements before taking their exam. Importantly RIAs, IARs, and CFP® professionals are fiduciaries, legally required to act in your best interest.

These fiduciary professionals are typically "fee-based," meaning they earn a fee or percentage of managed assets and may also receive commissions or fees on insurance products used in a comprehensive plan. They focus on the big picture and have all financial tools at their disposal.

SEEKING FINANCIAL ADVICE: BROKERS VS. FIDUCIARY INVESTMENT ADVISOR REPRESENTATIVES

Investors today can access two main types of financial advice: commission-based brokers who work for large banks and brokerage firms, or fee-based, independent fiduciary investment advisors. Unfortunately, many investors are unaware of the differences between these types of advice and the advisors who provide them. We went into some detail in a previous chapter however, here is some additional, information to help clear up any, confusion so you can find good advice from a professional you can trust:

The key difference between brokers, who fall under RegBI or the best interest standard of care that we discussed in Chapter 1 and registered investment advisors, and investment advisor representatives who are fiduciary, is that the latter are obligated to act in the investor's best interests ***in all aspects*** of the financial relationship. However, confusion still exists among investors trying to find the best and most credible financial advice.

Forbes cites some of the top reasons investors choose independent registered investment advisors (RIAs or IARs):*

- RIAs are fiduciaries and must offer advice in the client's best interest (in all aspects of the financial relationship).
- RIAs provide personalized service with transparent and competitive fees.
- Fee-based compensation, aligns the interest of the advisor and the client
- There is dissatisfaction with commission-based brokers.
- Access to institutional investments provides a robust array of investment choices.
- Newer technology enhances advisor-client engagement and communications.

---

* *2023 Forbes article by Shirl Penney*

Lastly, investment advisors abide by a code of ethics and provide their clients with a Form ADV describing the methods that the professional uses to do business.

Understanding your financial professional's role and title is crucial to retirement planning. While various professionals can assist with aspects of your finances, fiduciary financial professionals offer the most objective strategies and unbiased compensation. They can also guide non-financial aspects of your legacy and help develop tax-saving strategies.

1. Be Objective. At the end of the day, you need to separate the weak from the strong. You might want a strong personal rapport with your professional, or you may want to choose your professional for their personality, and positive attitude. What's most important is finding someone who can provide wise advice on achieving your retirement goals and has a proven track record of successfully guiding others on their retirement journey. Make sure they represent a firm that has the investment tools and products that you desire, and make sure they specialize in retirement income planning. That is, after all, the main goal.

Don't hesitate to investigate each candidate. Ask the same questions to compare them. Evaluate their credentials, experience, competence, ethics, fiduciary status, track record, and services.

Potential professionals should meet your qualifications in the following categories:

- **Credentials**: Consider their experience, education, professional associations, and certifications. Ongoing education and certifications ensure they're up to date on current financial practices.
- **Firm**: Choose a firm that as soon as you walk in, you feel welcomed from the get-go and with advisors operating under fiduciary standard. Evaluate candidates' track

record, compensation structure, reports, analyses, and added services. Get to know the rest of the firm's team, who will also be assisting you on your retirement planning journey. I've always said, "It's teamwork that makes the dream work."

- **Services**: Your Fiduciary Retirement Income Planner should specialize in retirement planning, not just accumulation. They should offer comprehensive services, including investment strategies, income planning, risk evaluation, insurance and annuities advice, and strategic tax planning.

- **References.** Every professional should provide at least two or three references. We like to offer references from clients who've been with us for 1-5 years, 5-10 years, and 10+ years to give prospective clients a range of experiences. Be cautious, as some references might be friends or colleagues, but a few good questions can uncover that. Contact references to check for inconsistencies, asking about their experience, relationship length, and satisfaction. While references are helpful, a strong track record and relevant experience matter more.

HOW TO INTERVIEW CANDIDATES

After vetting your candidates and narrowing down a list of professionals that you think might be a good fit for you, it's time to start interviewing.

When you meet in person with a professional, you want to take advantage of your time with them. The presentations and information that they share with you will be important to hear but you will also want to control some aspects of the interview. After a professional has told you what they want you to hear, it's time to ask your own questions to get the specific information you need to make your decision.

Make sure to prepare a list of questions and an informal agenda so that you can keep track of what you want to ask and what points you want the professional to touch on during the interview. Using the same questions and agenda will also allow you to more easily compare the professionals after you have interviewed them all. Remember that these interviews are just that, *interviews*. You are meeting with several professionals to determine with whom you want to work. But also realize that they are also determining if you will be a good fit for their firm and culture as well. Don't agree to anything or sign anything during an interview until after you have made your final decision.

It can also be helpful to meet them at their office. You can get a sense of the work environment, the staff culture and attitude, and how the firm does business.

You can use the following questions during an initial interview to get an understanding of how each professional does business and whether they are a good fit for you:

1. Are you a Fiduciary? How do you charge for your services? How much do you charge? Find out if they charge an initial planning fee, a percentage of assets under management, or earn commissions from selling financial products. Ask about specific costs to understand their incentives and ensure there are no surprises if you choose to work with them.

2. What are your credentials, licenses, and certifications? There are various financial professionals, such as CFPs, ChFCs, Investment Advisors, and CPAs. Choose someone with expertise relevant to your needs. If you're looking for investment management, seek an Investment Advisor. Independent firms often have teams of experts, like CPAs and CFPs. If you think a professional might be a good fit but lacks the accounting experience you need, ask about their firm's resources. If they work closely with experienced CPAs, it could still be a good match.

3. What are the financial services that you and your firm provide? The question within the question here is, "Can you help me achieve my goals?" Some people can only provide you with investment advice, some only offer insurance products and others are tax consultants. You will want to work with someone who provides a complete suite of financial planning services and products that touch on retirement planning, insurance options, legacy and estate structuring, and strategic tax planning.

4. What kinds of clients do you work with the most? A lot of financial professionals work within a niche: retirement income planning, investment planning, life insurance, etc. Finding someone who works with other people that are in the same "financial boat" as you and who have similar goals can be an important way to make sure they understand your needs. Do their strategies require a minimum level of investment? Ask where their expertise lies and decide whether or not their experience lines up with your needs.

5. How do you approach investing? Whether you're totally in the dark about investing or have some guiding principles, ask each candidate about their investment philosophy. Some approaches will resonate with you, while others won't. A reliable professional won't promise huge returns or claim they can make you a lot of money. Do they have a minimum asset requirement? Professionals who are successful at comprehensive retirement income planning and full-service investment management will listen to your goals, assess your risk tolerance, and understand your comfort level with different types of investment strategies. Trust is key, and this question will help you determine who's the right fit.

6. How do you stay in contact with your clients? Does your prospective professional hold annual or quarterly meetings? Does the firm engage clients throughout the year with events to build relationships? How often do you want to meet? Some prefer a yearly check-in to review everything, while others want to be more involved and understand their portfolio more often. Determine the level of involvement that works for you and your financial professional. Also, consider how they communicate, do you prefer phone calls, virtual, in-person meetings or are you open to all of the above?

7. Did they ask good questions and show signs that they were interested in working with me? A professional who structures your assets for a comfortable retirement must be a good listener. Avoid those who talk non-stop and dictate decisions without considering your needs. If they listen well, understand your goals, and show interest and experience in your situation, they may be a good fit.

THE IMPORTANCE OF INDEPENDENCE

Not all investment firms and financial professionals are created equally. This book highlights the need for modern, innovative strategies to leverage investments for income and accumulation in today's markets. No matter how good a financial professional is, the firm that they represent needs to operate on sound principles and offer strategies that make sense in today's economy. Remember, advice about money has been around forever. Relevant and appropriate advice, however, changes with the times.

For example, timing the market, relying on the sale of stocks for income and banking on high treasury and bond returns aren't realistic ways to make money or to generate income over long periods of time.

Working with an independent fiduciary can help you break free from outdated thinking and build a successful retirement income plan. A fiduciary who earns compensation based on your success brings peace of mind because when you do well, they do well. Also, they will make sure you know the steps to ensure:

- Your assets are organized and structured to reflect your risk tolerance.
- Your assets will be available to you when you need them and in the way that you need them.
- You will have a lifetime income that will support your lifestyle through your retirement.
- You create a tax efficient income plan.
- Your legacy and Estate Plan is in order.
- Your Red Money is complemented with Green and Yellow Money and is managed in your best interest.

Finding, interviewing, and selecting a financial professional can be daunting, but it's worth the effort. Your retirement, lifestyle, assets, and legacy are at stake, and the decisions you make now will have lasting effects. Trusting someone to act in your best interest is invaluable, and the time invested finding the right fiduciary firm and professionals is a decision you will not regret.

It's been said that **"The quality of our lives is often determined by the quality of our relationships"**. Commit to building strong connections, both professionally and personally, and take care to maintain a healthy body—because it's the only place you really have to live in on this earth.

The strongest retirements come from having something to retire to, not just from. Staying strong mentally, physically, financially, spiritually, and relationally—with friends, family, and faith—

leads to mental, emotional, and spiritual well-being, giving you the best chance for a fun and fulfilling retirement.

CHAPTER 15 QUICK TIPS //

- Choose fiduciary financial professionals who are legally obligated to act in your best interest throughout your retirement journey.

- Not all investment firms and financial professionals are created equally. Working with an independent fiduciary will give you more options that are customized to your unique set of circumstances.

- Invest the time to interview 2 to 3 retirement income planning firms and follow up on references given.

- To schedule a complimentary consultation with our fiduciary retirement income specialists, contact ETS Wealth Management at 770-904-1978 or info@etswealth.com.

Made in the USA
Columbia, SC
31 October 2024